DIVORCE
MAKING THE BREAK

D1119715

DIVORCE
MAKING THE BREAK

DAVID BELL

SILES PRESS LOS ANGELES

DissoMaster® reproduced by permission of the
California Family Law Report, Inc.

First Edition

10 9 8 7 6 5 4 3 2 1

Library of Congress Cataloging-in-Publication Data

Bell, David A., 1954-
Divorce : making the break / by David Bell. – 1st ed.
p.cm.
Includes bibliographical references.
1. Divorce. 2. Divorce–United States. I. Title.

HQ814 .B437 2002   306.89–dc21   2002017033

ISBN: 1-890085-06-5

Cover design by Heidi Frieder

Printed and bound in the United States of America

SILES
PRESS
3624 Shannon Road, Los Angeles, CA 90027

Dedicated to the children whose parents have parted

CONTENTS

PREFACE

Divorce is often painful, but it can be made excruciating when the separating spouses and family law professionals make poor choices during the divorce process. Divorce handled badly can cause enormous emotional and financial destruction to the parties involved—especially to children, the innocent bystanders.

On one hand, I hope this book will ease your fears about divorce; a "good divorce" that results in greater happiness for all concerned (yes, even the children) is actually possible.

On the other hand, I hope this book will *instill* fear in you about the destructive elements of the family law system so you can avoid them.

The choices you make during the divorce process will resonate forever in your life and the lives of your children and their other parent. I hope this book will help you to make constructive choices in divorce, to proceed in a positive manner, and to heal.

In stressful times, everything in life becomes intensified. When life challenges us, we learn the essence of our individual being. This discovery can be a great gift.

As you proceed with your divorce, remember that you have only a finite number of days on this earth. These days are best spent in creativity and happiness, states that are life-affirming.

Keep your moral center during this volatile time. Your integrity—your purity of intent—cannot be taken from you. It is yours to keep or give away by choice.

ACKNOWLEDGEMENTS

I am grateful to dozens of kind friends and family who listened (and listened and listened) to me, advised me, challenged me, and supported me as I emotionally processed through my own divorce and custody issues over the years. They have blessed my life immeasurably with their wisdom and caring.

Thanks especially goes to those who, in addition to extending the above-mentioned emotional support, patiently read (and diplomatically commented on) the early drafts of this book: Elizabeth Dohrman, Karen Salk, Jackie Iverson, Jay Gruska, Terri Potts, Richard Rintoul, David Howard, Bradley Wigor, Gail Eichenthal, and my anonymous friend in the east.

I am indebted to Linda Price; her love, patience, and sense of humor helped me weather the storms of divorce.

Special gratitude goes to Dr. Denise Mandel for wise, compassionate guidance during a long journey.

I owe enormous thanks to Dr. Mary Lund for her professional guidance and insights regarding custody issues (and life in general), to Gwen Feldman and Jim Fox of Siles Press for believing in and publishing this book, to Patricia Connell for editing the manuscript with dedication and sensitivity, to Mike Chesler for efforts beyond the call of duty, to Rosa Barrios for never wavering in her commitment to our family, to Marcia Weber and Dennis Risch for their help with family law information.

One of the positive aspects of my divorce experience was getting to know Lance Spiegel, an attorney who sets the standard for legal skill and high ethics. I am forever indebted to him for ensuring that I was able to be closely involved in my daughter's life. There is no greater gift he could have given me. As is common in high-conflict divorce, on numerous occasions I was tempted to indulge in legal extremes out of frustration and anger at a family law system that is often dysfunctional. Lance was always able to find the right words to diplomatically convince me to stay on a constructive track and channel my behavior in a manner that I wouldn't regret in the future. Now as I look back on the years of my divorce, I'm keenly aware what an important gift this also was.

Finally, I am most blessed by the miracle of parenthood and the privilege of witnessing the life of my daughter, Katie, who sets the standard for kindness, joy, and courage.

INTRODUCTION

On the morning of February 1, 1995, my five-month-old son died.

Andrew was a sweet, gentle soul whose neuromuscular circuitry simply didn't develop properly *in utero*. His short life was a steady decline from birth as his mother and I watched helplessly, desperately seeking a solution the medical community wasn't able to provide.

I've been told that the loss of a child may be the most stressful and emotionally painful event in the human experience.

I believe this to be true.

In recent years, I've been told by several knowledgeable people that the divorce rate for couples who lose a child is estimated to be eighty to ninety percent. Although many people might assume tragedy would bring a couple closer together, this statistic must measure something about human nature.

In the year following our son's death, my wife and I participated in intensive marital counseling. We also endured the second of two miscarriages. In March of 1996, my wife said she couldn't continue in the marriage. Perhaps I was only a few months away from saying those same words to her; we were both emotionally spent.

There is a point in a relationship when, for one or both parties, an emotional switch in the heart gets flipped to "off"; no recovery is possible. Further cohabitation only results in increased anger, resentment, and hostility.

I've been told that divorce is also one of the most stressful events in the human experience.

I believe this to be true, too.

When my wife told me of her decision, we stood in the kitchen and quietly, sadly told each other that we were sorry for the loss of the marriage. We made agreements about sharing custody of our four-year-old daughter and the equitable division of finances. The three of us had experienced a lot of trauma during the previous two years, and it was important that the divorce be as easy as possible on all of us, especially on our daughter.

Unfortunately, our shared-parenting agreement didn't hold, and, as happens in many divorces, the issue of joint child custody quickly became a point of high conflict.

I've been told that a child custody battle is also one of the most stressful and emotionally painful events in the human experience.

I believe this to be true as well.

A custody battle is about the potential loss of a child. However, there is the added pain of that loss being initiated by the other parent—it can be the ultimate betrayal.

The emotions of panic, fear, helplessness, and desperation I felt at the thought of losing regular and frequent contact with my daughter were strikingly similar to those I felt as I witnessed my son's slow decline and death.

Fortunately, in my case, a full-blown child custody evaluation and court ruling was averted and a shared-parenting agreement regarding the care of our daughter was negotiated through attorneys after a few months. But the custody conflict had caused the attorneys to become heavily involved, and mistrust and anger permeated all aspects of the divorce. As a result, many other issues spiraled out of control, and the divorce became a nightmare.

The divorce cost my ex-wife and me more than $250,000 plus three years of excruciating, nonstop, mind-numbing stress. It is a divorce that could have—and should have—cost only a few thousand dollars and taken a few months.

The irony is that the final custody arrangement, support payments, and division of assets set by the attorneys' negotiations and the judges' rulings ended up being exactly what my wife and I had verbally agreed upon in our kitchen conversation two years before.

This high-conflict, overlitigated divorce risked the financial security and emotional and physical health of my young daughter, the mother of my daughter, and me.

It has been a path of slash-and-burn destruction. In-law relationships are severed. Former mutual friends have either had to take sides or limit contact with both my ex-wife and me. My daughter's teachers, doctors, and schoolmates' parents are cautious around both of us. The level of parental conflict was such that it will probably always be a part of my daughter's life. It was not the legacy I had wished for her.

Tragically, my divorce experience is not unique.

I believe my experiences over the past few years qualify me to share life lessons of divorce, tragedy, grief, and recovery, so I am adding one more voice to the discussion about divorce with the hope that it will make a positive difference. I've had a firsthand look at a process that, under the best of circumstances, is painful. Under the worst of circumstances, it is destructive in ways I never imagined possible.

I'm not an attorney; nothing in this book should be taken as legal advice. Nor am I a mental health professional; the emotional and child-development advice in the text is what the experts generally agree will give you and your children the best chance for a positive, fulfilling life after divorce.

There are few absolutes in law or mental health; life is many shades of gray. Likewise, each divorce is different. However, recent research is clearly showing which behavior is most likely to have a positive result for divorcing spouses and their children. I urge you to play the odds and use the advice of the experts as a starting point for discussions, then make adjustments to suit your own family's situation. For instance, begin with an agreement in principle about a shared-parenting arrangement, then negotiate around work and school schedules so that each parent shall be with the child at least forty percent of the time. (Many family law professionals prefer the term "shared parenting" to "joint custody.")

Keep in mind that, over the years, you and your divided family will likely go through many changes that result in periodic upheaval. The future may hold remarriage; new stepsiblings for your children; a parent's move to a different, perhaps distant, locale; severe illness. Such inevitable challenges are all the more reason why the beginning of a divorce is the time to set a constructive tone for communicating and negotiating with your ex-spouse.

Most people going through divorce occasionally make poor choices in behavior, express anger in inappropriate ways, are less-than-ideal parents. I hope this book will help you identify destructive behavior in divorce and sensitize you to the impact your actions have on your children so you may minimize harmful choices.

If you are entering a divorce, this book is a personal plea to you—a plea to keep your moral integrity, to seek peace, to put your children first. Accomplishing these three goals while being tossed about in the emotional storm of divorce requires great effort.

When my divorce began, I drove to the bookstore to search for a few titles that I hoped would give me guidance for the unknown journey I was about to begin. Like most people going through bad times, I wanted to feel better quickly. I was depleted and didn't have the emotional resources left to filter through large volumes of text based on research studies or that dealt with only one component of divorce or that reflected the author's gender bias. I wanted to find a comprehensive but succinct overview of what was about to happen to my family. This is the book I wish I had found on the bookshelf that day. This is the book I wish all couples would read when they make the decision to separate.

This book includes very few details about my own divorce. It is a glimpse into the maw of the family law system, certainly based on my own experience to a degree, but largely based on hundreds of conversations and interviews with friends and acquaintances who have experienced divorce recently as adults or years ago as children of divorcing parents. These people were a treasure trove of guidance and wisdom for me. In many ways, this book is about their stories, for in listening to their divorce experiences, I have found most of them to have common patterns.

I do not discuss the extreme circumstances of divorce such as physical abuse, stalking, or kidnapping. This is a book for "normal" people caught up in emotionally volatile events, who, through thoughtful, conscious effort, are capable of limiting the number of poor choices they make.

This volume discusses divorce in general but is child-centered. When a child is conceived, a sacred covenant is made between two adults that the child will be best served by the balance and contrasting gifts offered by their feminine and masculine natures. Except in extreme circumstances, children need frequent and regular contact with both parents so they may learn from these differing styles.

It is most important that each parent pledge never to say anything derogatory about the other parent in the presence of a child, for doing so is emotionally damaging. Mother and father must selflessly put aside their own negative feelings about each other; we honor our children by making this commitment.

This is also intended to be a book about healing. If divorce causes you confusion and emotional pain, you are normal. In most cases, healing from divorce is not easy. It involves painful self-examination, unpleasant choices, the giving up of former dreams and hopes, and their replacement with new ones. It requires patience to let the whole process take place. Grief, confusion, and emotional turmoil associated with events such as divorce can last a long time.

Healing is being able to discover—and embrace—the positive aspects of life after divorce.

There are no shortcuts in a grieving/healing process. It's common for people to seek emotional comfort in the abuse of alcohol, drugs, sex, eating, shopping—even the abuse of seemingly healthy activities such as exercise or religious practice. But true healing can only come by acknowledging the loss, experiencing the sadness and turmoil over time, then slowly rebuilding your new life in a constructive way. It is not a neat, orderly process. It is often a faltering, stumbling, "two-steps-forward, one-step-back" kind of thing.

The most constructive—and healing—thing I did during my divorce and custody conflict was to seek information and guidance from friends and therapists, many of whom had experienced divorce in the past. I will always be grateful to them—they kept me on a good path, helped me find ways to avoid conflict and, when conflict was unavoidable, helped me cope with it.

While I've tried to minimize them, this book does contain some gender generalizations, many of which are based on societal conventions (for instance, the mom is usually the primary caretaker of the children, the dad is usually the primary wage-earner). Fortunately, gender roles are becoming more flexible.

I have tried to remove gender identification from my descriptions of divorcing parents. As you read the true stories in this book, you may try to guess if it was a father or mother who did such and such. In fact, virtually every act I've described has been done by both.

Neither gender can claim a monopoly on moral behavior. For every "deadbeat dad" who financially abandons his family, it wouldn't take much effort to find an equal number of moms who make false allegations of sexual or physical abuse against a father to gain sole custody of their children or strategic advantage in litigation (although these women have thus far evaded an equivalently catchy alliterative moniker, such as "malicious mom").

Fortunately, governments are beginning to take steps to create accountability for these wrongs. Federal, city, and state governments are cooperating in tracking down spouses who are delinquent in paying child support; in the state of California, making a false allegation of child abuse in connection with custody proceedings is a felony.

In this book I am sometimes harsh with the professionals in the family law system. I must balance that by saying that I know of many heroes—ethical attorneys, therapists, mediators, judges—who, year after year, work within a divorce system that deals with an ugly and destructive side of human behavior. They exist in a world where there are no winners; it is a landscape of losses. At best, they witness torrents of "he said/she said" whining and blaming. At worst, they witness unimaginable spousal and child abuse.

Unless your divorce is very amicable and your financial situation is very simple, I highly recommend some degree of involvement by an ethical family law professional. I have heard it said that it is possible to file your own divorce and also possible to cut your own hair, but doing either carries great potential for an unhappy result.

Even if you retain attorneys and accountants, it is crucial that you and your soon-to-be-ex-spouse communicate directly or through a mediator to keep the family law professionals from escalating the hostilities. Later in this book you will find guidance in helping you choose an ethical attorney.

Legal documents can be intimidating. For this reason, I have included several in the Appendix so you may know what to expect. For definitions of legal terms in family law, refer to books such as *Nolo's Pocket Guide to Family Law* (Nolo Press) or *The American Bar Association Guide to Family Law* (Times Books).

In most cases, the divorce turmoil will eventually settle down. It will probably take two or three years after a divorce is finalized for most of the healing process to be completed. This is why finalizing the divorce as quickly as possible and setting up a cooperative shared-parenting relationship with your ex-spouse should be your main goals—and the goals of your attorney. An ethical attorney will promote this even though it may not be what you want to hear. (Throughout the divorce process, keep in mind that an ethical attorney will tell you the painful truth, but an unethical attorney will tell you what you want to hear; more about this later.)

I do not believe there is such a thing as winning in the family-court system. Perhaps it should be viewed more as minimizing your losses. In divorce there are many losses, both emotional and material. You will need to compromise on many issues, and it will probably be painful. Divorce is the dismantling of a union or partnership that took years of love and effort to create—it is the end of something that was dear to you at one time.

However, divorce can also bring hope. Hope is one of the most crucial elements in human existence, and, in a bad marriage, there is very little of it.

You now have a chance to build a new life.

FIRST CONSIDERATIONS

[This is] a world in which people are capable of immense cruelty to each other. There is war, there is crime, there is fraud, there is murder, there is rape. What does God want me to do about it? What I learned is: God created the world with people free to choose good or evil so that there would be the possibility of people choosing good.

What I believe is that the most precious thing in the sight of God is the good deed freely chosen.

This is a world where people can as easily choose to be mean and vicious as they can choose to be good. In fact, sometimes it's easier to be mean. There seems to be a moral law of gravity that pulls us down. That makes it easier to lie than tell the truth when the truth is embarrassing. That makes it easier to be selfish than to be generous.

We need to believe that the universe cares if we are good or bad, if we are truthful.

— from a televised PBS interview with Rabbi Harold S. Kushner, author of *When Bad Things Happen to Good People*

BREAKING THE MARITAL CONTRACT

A marriage is a series of innumerable daily contracts between partners. When we analyze the layers of a marital relationship, it's remarkable how complicated the coexistence really is.

As individuals, we need a safe, supportive emotional and physical environment that allows us to grow. Each of us has a strong will to shape and control our life environment.

All group dynamics—whether in a corporation, a sports team, or a marriage—have an inherent tension between the needs/wants of the individual and the needs/wants of the group or partnership. Finding an appropriate balance between them can be difficult.

Almost every minute of married life represents a negotiated contractual agreement with a spouse—our job, our house, the car we drive, how money is earned and spent, which side of the bed we sleep on, where our toothbrush and comb are stored.

A surprising number of these are unspoken contracts that just evolve into the fabric of daily life. And, being unspoken, they may not be good contracts but are assumptions that each partner has about the marriage. Assumptions are often a result of poor communication—one partner can assume that the other has entered into a contract when the other has no clue that a contract existed.

Many of these assumptions may be carryovers from the family life each partner experienced as a child (Dad maintained the house and car; Mom was primary child-care provider) and may not have a major effect on the partnership. However, other assumptions may indeed have a negative impact on the partnership.

Throughout the marriage, each partner has a conscious or unconscious list of which marital contracts (and assumptions) he/she would like to see remain intact and which he/she would like to see change over time. These lists may not be the same for both partners.

As the years go by, the contracts that were clearly articulated and understood by both parties face the test of changing times and changing life situations. The assumptions face the test of becoming clearly defined (and sometimes surprising) realities—or the assumptions may never be clearly defined. For many people, these changes, clearly defined realities, or lack of resolution create conflicts that can become intolerable.

The marital contract is broken.

Marital contracts come in different shapes and sizes.

Small broken contracts can begin to accumulate and cause stress on the marriage. The bemused tolerance we exhibited at the start of the marriage about her not putting her shoes in the closet, him leaving the toilet seat up, her not changing the oil in her car, him watching sports on television may, over years, change to resentment and begin to take a toll.

The next level of broken contracts is more serious: promises to stop smoking, to get and keep a job, to curtail excessive spending, to spend more time with the family, to communicate with each other, to commit one's energies, love, and dedication to the marriage and the family.

The most severe level of breaking the marital contract involves such things as sexual infidelity, drug or alcohol abuse, emotional or physical abuse, addictive gambling or addictive spending of the family money, withholding love and support in times of personal tragedy. These are difficult to overcome.

Not all marital changes or broken contracts are entirely negative or ill-intentioned. What one spouse regards as growth or change, the other spouse may feel is betrayal. For example, one partner may make drastic changes in employment choices, religious beliefs, life philosophies, definitions of intimacy, even changes in declared sexual identity.

And sometimes chaotic life events completely out of our control can destroy a marriage.

Hopefully, you will examine your life choices and motivations at some point in the future to learn how much you contributed to the breakdown of the marriage so you can minimize those traits in future relationships. But in the midst of divorce, you may be too depleted to do an accurate and constructive self-assessment.

Was it a mistake to marry that person? Perhaps in hindsight the answer is obvious; the clues may have been there when you were dating. Perhaps you thought your spouse would eventually change and see life the way you do (that he/she would watch less television and spend more time in family activities, for instance). Or perhaps you thought that, over the years, he/she would learn to trust you and become intimate. Perhaps there were little difficulties that, at the beginning of the relationship, you brushed off with "no one's perfect"—but something became intolerable for one or both.

The reality is that you made the best choices you could with the tools you had at that time in your life. Perhaps romantic intoxication also played a significant part.

Most likely the marriage/divorce experience has created pain and burden for you. But perhaps it provided you with beautiful children or emotional maturity. Very often a painful experience presents us a gift if we are open to it.

For more on marital contracts, read the book *Crazy Time* by Abigail Trafford. While it's an excellent discussion of divorce, I would recommend it to anyone *entering* a love relationship. In fact, I believe parts of it should be required reading in high school "life skills" classes.

FIRST CHOICES

As the reality of separation and divorce set in, you may experience a whirlwind of emotions: disbelief, anger, sorrow, shame. You may also experience symptoms typical of mild depression: lack of concentration, bouts of crying, fatigue. You may even experience relief. While in this emotional maelstrom, you must make some of the most important choices of your life.

The choices you make during the divorce process may set the tone for many years—perhaps forever—of your dealings with your ex-spouse. In the future, you will need to cooperate with the other parent of your children; now is the time to create an environment that makes this possible.

This is a time when your humanity and morality will be tested, a time that will define your character. It is easy to be moral when life is flowing smoothly. You must look beyond the pain and turmoil of the moment and make choices that will best serve you, your children—and, yes, their other parent—in the long run.

You know your estranged spouse's weaknesses, his or her most vulnerable spots. You can choose to use this knowledge as a weapon in legal paperwork and court filings, or you can act with restraint. It is one of the moral challenges you will face in divorce.

As Judith Viorst notes in her excellent book *Necessary Losses*, "No two adults can do each other more damage than husband and wife."

This can be especially true in divorce.

The greatest challenges in divorce are to:

(1) clearly define goals that have integrity (for instance, minimizing the negative impact of the divorce on your children, keeping parent/child relationships intact and healthy, not using your life energy to punish or harass your ex);

(2) figure out how to achieve those goals with the least conflict and least expense.

It's beneficial to use these two points as a framework for decision-making and for discussions with your attorney if you retain one. The clarity and communication achieved in these conversations will help your case in many ways.

Stay focused and keep your eyes on the prize. Do not allow yourself to be knocked off course by your own negative behavior and emotions, your ex-spouse's negative behavior and emotions, or the weaknesses of the family law system. Think before acting.

Exercise restraint. React slowly to conflicts with your ex-spouse. Try to keep your interactions on a "strictly business" level until you are able to handle closer ties. Take time to cool off if you are placed in an emotionally volatile situation. ("I'd rather continue this discussion when our emotions are not so high. I promise to call you tomorrow.") Hot-button issues may need to be dealt with in mediation and/or counseling.

Many of the issues that seem absolutely crucial to you during the emotionally charged period at the beginning of a divorce will have little or no importance in a year or so.

You've spent a lifetime observing and discussing other people's good and bad moral choices when they've been in conflict. Now it's your turn—you are in the spotlight. Your friends, your family, your children, the teachers and doctors who care for your children will now be observing—and be affected by—the moral content of your choices.

In Bill Moyers' book *A World of Ideas*, the ethicist Michael Josephson states,

> An ethical person ought to do more than he's required to do and less than he's allowed to do. He must exercise judgment, self-restraint, and conscience. Otherwise, we have a minimalist society where everybody's lawyering everybody else, pushing the world to the limit, and twisting the rules.

To gauge the ethics of your choices, ask yourself questions like these:

➤ Are you keeping the divorce process businesslike, or are you using it as a forum for your rage?

➤ Are the choices you're making moral, ethical ones? Or are they hurtful, spiteful, vengeful?

➤ Are you using your child as a weapon or a bargaining chip?

➤ Are you making choices that follow the advice of divorce experts—advice that favors the odds of your children doing well after the dust settles?

➤ In ten or twenty years, will you want your children to read the court papers you have filed against your ex-spouse?

➤ In ten or twenty years, will you be proud of your actions when you look back on them?

11

Humans sometimes have the unsettling ability to justify their poor choices and immoral behavior. To cite an extreme example, after World War II, Nazi soldiers justified their war crimes with "I was obeying orders."

Many people justify immoral choices every day: "The cashier gave me too much change. Since it's the cashier's mistake, I am justified in keeping the money." Or "My spouse had an affair, so it's okay if I have one." Or "It's only considered cheating if you get caught. Everybody does it."

In divorce, immoral choices can be justified by statements such as "I wrote those awful things about my ex-spouse in the court papers because my attorney said I should" or "I accused my ex-spouse of abuse because that's how divorce litigation is done—I had to do it to them before they did it to me." This is the morality of the unethical client or unethical attorney who believes that the end justifies the means.

Litigants may also use aggressive or unethical tactics out of fear; they've never been through high-conflict litigation before. They can easily be persuaded by an attorney who does the maximum in the case to (1) protect himself or herself against any accusations of misrepresentation a client may make or (2) make more money.

You can—and must—do better than this. Once you lose your moral center with distortions or lies, especially those that harm another person, you can never get it back in a whole, pristine piece. To paraphrase an old saw, once a sapling gets a bend in its trunk, the mature tree will never be perfectly straight.

It may be difficult to resist the temptation to use attorneys and courts to punish your ex-spouse, teach him or her a lesson, empower yourself, act out your rage at the world, and grab custody of your children.

In his book *From Courtship to Courtroom*, attorney Jed H. Abraham criticizes divorce law:

> Divorce law plays off married couples as adversaries; it expects they will get champion attorneys to realize their rights. Attorneys are trained to fight hard for their clients. These ingredients, when mixed with the heightened emotions of shame, rage, fear, and vengefulness that accompany virtually all contested divorces, place implacable pressure on the fragile virtues of modesty, restraint, politeness, and accommodation.

It may be difficult to stay on a moral path when you feel compelled to fight fire with fire; it's easy to become convinced that your ex-spouse's accusations will gain credence unless you rebut each with one of your own. Each of us has plenty of intimate ammunition to use against our ex-spouse.

It feels risky if one doesn't play by the unwritten rules of family law: attack and retaliate. After all, what can you lose by staking out extreme positions around financial or custody matters in the hope that you'll end up with something more than if you'd made only reasonable requests?

The current family law system too often allows this scenario to be part of the divorce landscape.

When caught up in the anger and fear of divorce,

➤ it can be more difficult not to attack or retaliate with betrayals of marital intimacies;

➤ it can be more difficult not to distort facts to gain strategic advantage in litigation;

13

➤ it can be more difficult not to stake out exaggerated financial positions;

➤ it can be more difficult to stay committed to a shared-parenting arrangement and not petition the court for primary custody of your children.

FEAR

While the divorce process is often driven by the anger and frustration of the parties involved, fear is a primary factor that motivates people to make destructive choices during this period of their lives.

Fear is a reaction to the unknown. The family law system too often instills fear instead of allaying it.

The three biggest fears in "normal" divorce—which are discussed individually below—involve

(1) child custody arrangements,

(2) financial security,

(3) facing life as a divorced person.

Unethical attorneys prey on these fears to acquire and keep clients by saying or implying things like, "If you don't file for sole custody of your children, you might not even get *joint* custody."

All attorneys must occasionally use fear as a technique to apply pressure to the opposing side—it is inherent in litigation. However, unethical attorneys routinely capitalize on fear as a litigation and negotiation weapon against the other spouse; preying on fear is a main tool of their trade.

This is also why I believe that mediators and therapists need to play a larger role in the family law system. They are generally more inclined to promote communication, clarity, healing, and solutions to assuage the fears of the parties involved, so that fear doesn't become a driving force and create a destructive divorce.

If a couple locked in a high-conflict divorce is required to meet several times with a mediator, review the divorce laws and the process of dividing financial assets, and learn most-likely outcomes both with and without litigation, they will be more likely to make constructive decisions. Knowledge can minimize fear.

Virginia, Utah, Connecticut, and New Hampshire have passed legislation that requires divorcing parents to attend parent-education classes to sensitize them about how their behavior during and after the divorce will impact their children. (This has been such a success in Utah that eighty percent of the attendees believe that a similar program *before* marriage would be helpful.*)

(1) CHILD CUSTODY ARRANGEMENTS

Certainly parent/child bonding is a prime consideration, but child custody arrangements are, in large part, about the oversight and control of the children's daily life.

For most parents, the thought of shared-custody arrangements that result in not seeing their children every day is extremely difficult. While we expect our children to leave home and live in other houses, apartments, or college dorms when they reach their late teens, most of us aren't emotionally prepared for it to happen when they are in the elementary grades or even preschool.

This early departure from the nest can be difficult even when the divorce and custody negotiations have been amicable. However, when

---

* *Speak Out for Children* (Children's Rights Council newsletter),
Summer/Fall 1999

they become highly conflictive, the fear of "losing" custody, of seeing their children infrequently or not at all, of the other parent moving thousands of miles away, can make people crazy—in some cases quite literally.

One of the reasons people stay in unhappy marriages is so they can continue to have daily contact with, or oversight of, their children. The possibility of losing this daily connection is too high a price to pay in order to pursue their own personal happiness as a divorced person.*

This daily oversight, involvement with—and care of—our children is an expectation with which we have been programmed our whole lives. As children, playing house with the boy or girl next door and acting out parenting roles, we were learning and rehearsing the covenant of caring for our future children.

It can be excruciating to reprogram ourselves to accept the fact that our young children will not be with us for days at a time and may be in the half-time care of someone we don't entirely trust—i.e., if the other parent were a babysitter, we'd fire him or her.

In most cases, it gets easier as everyone gradually adjusts to the new living arrangements. After a year or so, you may wonder how you, your children, and your ex-spouse ever lived together in a house fraught with tension.

Sometimes spouses will seek full custody of a child because they are unable to give up control. These may be "control freaks" disguised as concerned parents who cannot stand the thought of someone else

---

*I heard a firsthand story about a couple who chose to stay together "for the sake of the children"; they agreed to delay their divorce until the youngest child turned eighteen years old. While the merits of this decision could be debated, it became insidious because they told their adolescent children of their decision. This placed an emotional burden on the children: They were now responsible for prolonging their parents' unhappy marriage.

caring for their child, bathing their child, selecting clothing for their child, feeding their child in a manner other than the way they want it to be done.

Then there are the emotionally insecure parents who cannot stand the thought of the other parent loving "their" child—or of the other parent receiving love from "their" child. They may be especially threatened if the ex-spouse is a good parent.

(2) FINANCIAL SECURITY

Divorce has negative consequences on the financial security of both parties, which can result in drastic changes in lifestyle. The income earned to support one household must now support two.

From *Crazy Time* by Abigail Trafford:

> One of the biggest shocks of divorce is financial: You're a lot poorer than you were before. It doesn't seem fair; to suffer so emotionally and then to suffer financially just when it would be nice to have some extra money to help you ease your way through the trauma. If you're a man and worked for twenty years to have the good life, perhaps you're now renting a furnished efficiency apartment; back where you were when you started, and what with child support you think you'll be lucky if you ever have a decent place to live. If you're a woman who's been primarily a homemaker for the last fifteen years, you find you can't even get credit, let alone a job. How are you supposed to go to work when there's nothing you know how to do, and besides, who's going to take care of the children when they come home from school? Life takes on a very grim edge.

The threat of being left financially ruined can motivate one or both parents to play out their primal fears through litigation. One or both of the litigants can lose their moral center in the fear.

Money issues are often used to punish the other litigant or are the source of fear regarding basic survival. Too often, clients spend $10,000 in attorney fees trying to acquire $1,000 more from their ex-spouse. (I've heard this referred to as "burning the barn to cook an egg.")

An attorney friend once told me:

> My observation is that far too much money in matrimonial litigation is spent on determining what the marital estate consists of, whereas the real and important issue for the parties' and children's ongoing well-being is how the marital estate should be divided. Rarely in my experience is there a big payoff for expending large sums to determine what assets there are. Divorcing spouses probably know most of what there is to know about their and their spouse's financial condition, and it usually isn't worth the extra money to find out what little they don't know. Unfortunately, saying the words "I want a divorce" doesn't create new assets, but it often needlessly dissipates the ones you have.

In many cases, spousal-support and child-support payments aren't as negotiable as litigants are led to believe. Most states have clear-cut formulas for financial issues such as support and have adopted computer software programs that, by comparing the incomes of both parties, determine guideline support payments to the dollar (see examples in Appendix).

I hope the chapters on finance at the end of this book will clarify the process, minimize your fears, and eliminate unnecessary litigation for you.

(3) FACING LIFE AS A DIVORCED PERSON

Most of us have been intensely programmed—virtually every day of our lives—to move toward the goal of marriage and creating a family. We learn this from our parents, friends, and relatives, from movies and books, even from popular songs.

When we marry, we invest that past—those expectations, hopes, and dreams—into the partnership. We also invest our future hopes and dreams: Everything we plan for our future now includes our partner. We have, in a sense, invested our whole self into this partnership.

One day we wake up and find ourselves alone—our worst nightmare has come true. We feel panic, tightness, despair, blood-draining-from-our-face disbelief. ("This can't really be happening!")

We are facing another unknown in life and can react with fear and confusion. It may feel like an emotional free fall. The stress may be compounded because we are no longer able to get support from our partner, who, in the past, may have helped us through other life crises. And not only are we facing the fears alone, but our ex-spouse may intentionally be causing us harm in litigation and intentionally using our fears as a litigation tactic against us.

The sense of loneliness may be intensified if, as is common, our married friends withdraw from us. Not only are we now a "fifth wheel," but we are a living example that their worst nightmare can come true (and it might be contagious).

Reprogramming our inner souls to accept being single can take time. It requires support and love from friends and family. It requires guidance and reassurance from people who have been down the path before us. Knowing that the emotional turmoil we're experiencing is normal and knowing what to expect in the ensuing months and years can be a big help emotionally—and a big help in making better choices at the beginning of the divorce process.

Divorce is a huge loss. You may experience phases of grief similar to those of people who lose a loved one through death.

From Judith Viorst's book *Necessary Losses*:

> The breakup of a marriage is a loss like the death of a spouse, and will often be mourned in closely parallel ways. There are some important distinctions: Divorce evokes more anger than death, and it is, of course, considerably more optional. But the sorrow and pining and yearning can be as intense. The denial and despair can be as intense. The guilt and self-reproach can be as intense. And the feeling of abandonment can be even more intense—"He didn't have to leave me; he chose to leave me."
>
> According to recent studies, the costs of divorce—both the physical costs and the emotional ones—can be higher than those imposed by a spouse's death.
>
> I have heard many women say—I've heard a few men say it too—that they would have rather been widowed than divorced, that death would not have entangled them in continuing fights over property and children, in feelings of jealousy, in feelings of failure.

Divorce hurts. Recovery will be slow. It will be one hour at a time, then one day at a time, then a week, then a month. A year or two after the divorce is finalized, you will probably find yourself back on your feet and moving forward.

In three to five years, you will likely wonder how you could ever have chosen to marry your ex-spouse. In five to ten years, it is not uncommon for ex-spouses to marry new partners and to be able to socialize together at their child's birthday party in a friendly manner.

21

Personal therapy can bring some relief. Therapy is often about articulating and clarifying a situation—this clarity and knowledge can shine light into the dark unknowns that cause us fear. Therapy can help us define our unhealthy life patterns, especially in personal relationships. Through conscious, thoughtful effort, it can give us a better chance of making healthy choices.

Other things that may help you cope are divorce support groups, books, exercise, yoga, new friends, classes, and volunteer work. You need to redefine yourself as a single person. You need to do it without the false support of "feeling better" with alcohol, drugs, or a quick new rebound relationship.

"WINNING" CUSTODY

The family law system is permeated with the fear of one parent "winning" custody, and with the perception that custody is an all-or-nothing issue.

This win/loss threat—real or implied—is too often used as a litigation tactic and distorted to a degree that is harmful to all parties involved. It is particularly ugly when child custody matters are used as leverage to negotiate financial matters.

The family law system could dispel the fear of losing contact with a child and discourage the abuse of child custody laws by mandating a long-term, rarely flexible commitment to shared parenting. The issue would not be *if* joint custody happens, but *how* it happens. Recent studies show that states that have legislated presumption of joint custody experience lower divorce rates.

"Joint custody" or "shared parenting" does not necessarily mean an exact fifty/fifty time-sharing of the children. Many unique, customized, shared-parenting plans are created by parents who are willing to work together in the best interests of the child. These ensure that, unless there is genuine risk to the child, each parent will spend significant time with the child and will have a say in important issues such as medical needs, education choices, summer camp, and so on.

The concept of "winning" children in a contest (albeit a legal one) categorizes them as objects. This in itself is one of the most immoral elements of the family law system.

This ugly concept is perpetuated in the terminology used by attorneys and parents: "I got my client custody of the children" or "I have the children on alternate weekends." Words such as "got" and "have" should be used to refer to possessions, not human beings.

Please consider using phrases such as, "My son stays at my house Sundays through Wednesdays" or "My daughter is with me the first half of each week" or "I will be with her next weekend." This difference in terminology is important: It honors our children as human beings, not as objects to be possessed. It sets the tone for how we approach all custody issues.

As parents, it is an honor and a privilege for parents to be with our children, to watch them grow, to share their thoughts and emotions, to offer them as many new life experiences as we can so they may choose those that suit them best.

Here's what may happen if you make an unwarranted grab for primary custody of your child, if you try to limit and control the other parent's access:

Your chances of success are small if the other parent is determined to be involved in the life of the child and decides to fight you on this issue. Slowly but surely, more and more legislatures and courts are inclined to presume joint custody. If that cannot be worked out, there may be a "nudge from the judge," who will punish the parent who tries to limit the other parent's access to the child by granting majority custody to that second parent. In other words, your strategy may backfire.

The hostility between you and your ex-spouse may escalate quickly and severely. Any semblance of trust that existed between the two of you may be destroyed for a long time. This will probably result in a breakdown of communication and cooperation. This is not what your child needs; children need peace and stability to progress and grow. Child-development experts agree that there is a direct link between the level of parental conflict and the negative emotional impact divorce has on children.

Your child will be placed in the middle of a war, one that probably has little to do with the child but is a way the parents act out their anger at each other using the child as a weapon. This can become truly grotesque as one or both parents subtly brainwash or overtly coach the child to think of the other parent as incompetent, neglectful, or dangerous—perhaps with the hope that this may have some influence in a custody evaluation done by a mental health professional. Keep in mind that, if you are caught coaching a child in this manner, it may have negative consequences for you in the courts—and in how children view you in the future once they are old enough to learn the truth.

This war can result in emotional and financial devastation. Instead of conserving emotional and financial resources to help you heal, find a new home, create a healing environment for your child, and save for your child's college fund, you are wasting your limited money and energy on legal proceedings.

Extended family can become involved in the hostility by involvement in the litigation, by making derogatory remarks about the other parent within earshot of the child, or by erasing all reference to

25

the other parent in conversation, photos, and so forth. This is emotionally damaging to a child.

Your family and friends or the parents of your child's friends may become cautious. They may feel that they are being asked to choose sides, or they may limit contact with both parties so as not to become involved. This, too, damages the safe and supportive community environment for your child, and again, it's the child's loss.

Teachers, doctors, and other caretakers of your child may become cautious around you and and your ex-spouse. Your child's welfare is the first priority of these professionals, and they know that this means being able to cooperate and communicate with both parents. They may be cautious around all of you so that their professional relationship with your child cannot be used as a tool in the parents' litigation.

All of this may leave your child in an emotional free fall. The child's existence will be enveloped by hostility and mistrust; he or she is being used as a tool for expressing anger. Children know when they are a source of conflict and hatred rather than of love and honor. They become cautious, fearing that something they say may escalate hostilities between their parents. This is especially tragic, for childhood should be a time of feeling safe to express thoughts freely and openly.

SHARED PARENTING: LISTENING TO THE EXPERTS

*Children who suffer the most from their parents' separation
are those who have their relationship with one parent
disrupted by loss of contact with that parent.*
— Dr. Judith Wallerstein, coauthor of *Surviving the Breakup,
Second Chances,* and *The Good Marriage*

Mothers and fathers become separated from their children for various reasons. They may be victimized by an unfavorable custody ruling. They may desert children for selfish reasons—a new romance, for instance. Or they may distance themselves from the children because they have problems with mental health, physical abuse, or substance abuse.

We are beginning to realize what an important part *both* parents play in their children's development. The research done on divorced families overwhelmingly supports joint-custody arrangements. It is best if this shared parenting is amicable or, at the very least, civil and businesslike.

In his book *The Best Parent Is Both Parents*, David Levy summarizes numerous studies done on child custody. Among the findings:

➤ "Children in joint custody reported significantly more positive experiences than children in maternal custody. Self-esteem was higher for children in joint custody."

➤ "[Joint-custody] children had significantly fewer behavioral problems than did the sole-custody subjects. Sole-custody children had greater self-hate and perceived more rejection from their fathers than joint-physical-custody children."

➤ "Most single-parent children were found to be dissatisfied with the amount of visitation they had, whereas the joint-custody children were content with their arrangements."

➤ "The joint-custody children retained a normal parent-child relationship, whereas sole-custodial children had a relationship with their non-custodial parent similar to the relationship between a child and an aunt or uncle."

➤ "Joint-custody parents were less likely to feel over-burdened by parenting responsibilities as compared to sole-custody parents."

The Children's Rights Council, based in Washington, D.C., publishes a quarterly newsletter called *Speak Out for Children*. The summer/fall 1999 issue included an article titled "Why Kids Need Moms and Dads," which reports that:

➤ Seventy-two percent of Americans believe that fatherlessness is the most significant family or social problem facing America.

➤ Forty percent of the children of divorced parents haven't seen their dads in the last year.

➤ Thirty-six percent of children, approximately 24.7 million, don't live with their biological father. In 1960, just nine percent of children lived with one parent.

➤ The number of live births to unmarried women increased from 224,300 in 1960 to 1,248,000 in 1995, while the number of children living with never-married mothers grew from 221,000 in 1960 to 5,862,000 in 1995.

➤ A white teenage girl with an advantaged background is five times more likely to become a teen mom if she grows up in a household headed by a single mother than if she is raised by both her biological parents.

➤ Girls fifteen to nineteen raised in homes with fathers are significantly less likely to engage in premarital sex, and seventy-six percent of teenage girls surveyed said their fathers are very or somewhat influential over their decisions regarding sex.

➤ Girls raised in single-mother homes are more likely to give birth while single and more likely to divorce and remarry. Studies have shown that girls whose fathers depart before their fifth birthday are especially likely to have permissive sexual attitudes and to seek approval from others.

➤ Fatherless children are at dramatically greater risk of drug and alcohol abuse.

➤ When dads don't live with their kids, the children are 4.3 times more likely to smoke cigarettes when teenagers.

➤ Children with fathers are twice as likely to stay in school.

➤ Eighty-five percent of youths in prison are from fatherless homes.

➤ Paternal praise is associated with better behavior and achievement in school, while the father's absence increases vulnerability and aggressiveness in young children, particularly boys.

➤ Children living in households with fathers are less likely to suffer from emotional disorders and depression.

➤ Children with involved dads are less susceptible to peer pressure and are more competent, more self-protective, more self-reliant, and more ambitious.

A CONSTRUCTIVE DIVORCE

Below are four critical issues in achieving a constructive divorce:

(1) KEEP YOUR MORAL CENTER

Never forget that your integrity—purity of intent—cannot be taken from you. It is yours to give away by choice.

The greatest gift you can give yourself and your children is being able to walk away from your divorce with a clean heart knowing that you did not engage in dirty tricks, did not try to hurt or punish your child's other parent, did not betray marital intimacies to gain strategic advantage, did not use your children as bargaining chips or weapons.

You must assertively protect your personal interests, but without intent to cause pain or suffering to anyone else. Sometimes there is a fine line between assertiveness and aggressiveness, but a good attorney knows where that line is.

(2) PUT YOUR CHILDREN FIRST

No matter how much you may dislike your ex-spouse, commit to a cooperative joint child custody arrangement with the other parent (unless he or she is truly, genuinely a danger). Participate in co-parent counseling if need be, but create a workable shared-parenting arrangement. It is the moral obligation of the parents to communicate and cooperate regarding the children.

Some divorced parents resist communicating or cooperating with the other parent because they feel it is giving respect or accommodation the other parent doesn't deserve. This is not true. When you communicate and cooperate with the other parent, you are giving to your child.

You may have to co-parent through gritted teeth. It will only be for a few years; your children will grow up and won't require joint-parenting as adults. But keep in mind that you will be tied to your ex-spouse forever through milestones in your adult child's life.

As parents, we are instinctively programmed to throw ourselves in the path of danger to shield our children from physical harm—we will surrender our lives for the sake of our children. Yet too many divorcing parents are not willing to surrender their rage to shield their children from the emotional harm of a high-conflict divorce. This is a selfish choice.

32

In the decisions you make and in the behavior you choose to display, the impact on your child should be your primary concern. In every decision you make, ask yourself, "Will this benefit my child? Am I following the advice of child-development experts?" A child's emotional health, behavior, and progress in school and life will often be the litmus test for gauging the merits of the parents' decisions regarding custody and cooperative joint-parenting.

Children need civility and cooperation between their parents around home transitions, school activities, birthday parties, illness or injury, their wedding day. If occasions such as these—when both parents are present—create anxiety for a child, one or both of the parents may have made selfish choices and placed their own needs for anger or revenge ahead of the child's need for a peaceful, cooperative environment.

Your children will, on some level, know if you place your personal interests or your rage ahead of their needs. In the future, a child may be the harshest (and most astute) judge of your actions regarding custody and related financial matters.

A friend of mine whose parents divorced twenty years ago, when she was a teenager, told me, "The child's image of a parent can change dramatically when the child sees the parent acting like a jerk in divorce. There is a permanent loss of respect for the parent, a loss of faith because it's obvious that the parent doesn't have the child's best interests at heart."

Instruct everyone around your child—relatives, babysitters, friends—that they are never to say anything derogatory about the other parent in the child's presence.

Putting your children first may even mean turning down a better job offer in another city or state so your children may stay in close contact with both parents.

(3) AVOID LITIGATION

Exhaust mediation and joint-parenting counseling before involving courts and attorneys in litigation.

Use litigation only if your situation genuinely poses a physical, emotional, or financial threat to you or your children.

Once you are sucked into the vortex of the family law system, extricating yourself is difficult. You will lose control of decisions about your children and your financial future. Those decisions will be made by the professionals in the family law system. Not only are these professionals strangers to your family, but these people will likely make mistakes and errors in judgment. At best, they may impose cookie-cutter financial and custody arrangements on you.

The price of litigation will be high in both emotional and financial terms. It will be costly in ways you can't yet foresee.

If litigation is unavoidable, refrain from attacking your ex-spouse. Once the mudslinging starts, it may result in retaliation, the conflict will escalate, and litigation fees will spiral. You can easily find yourself in a high-conflict, prolonged divorce case. Once trust and cooperation are destroyed, the other parent may have difficulty confiding in you about particular problems in your child's life for fear that the confidence will someday be used against him/her as a weapon in litigation. Yet discussing and solving the negatives in your child's life in partnership with the other parent is crucial.

At the beginning of your divorce proceedings, you may think that a few lies and distortions won't matter, but the repercussions can be long-term and damaging in ways you cannot yet foresee. A good attorney knows ways to protect your interests without attacking or making distorted or false accusations against your ex-spouse.

34

(4) GET FREQUENT REALITY CHECKS

During the emotionally volatile time of divorce, it is fairly certain that your perceptions of the situation will not be accurate—you may be blinded by sadness, anger, and fear.

You may have people around you—divorced friends or an attorney—who will counsel you to attack or punish your spouse, to use the family law system to act out your personal rage or to gain strategic advantage by "doing it to them before they do it to you."

Keep in mind that they have their own agendas and their own histories, which will color their advice to you. These people may not have your best interests at heart.

Think back to your childhood. No doubt there were occasions when friends egged you on to take an ill-advised, risky action—one they would never take themselves despite their posturing to the contrary. Aging doesn't necessarily change human nature.

Seek advice from people who are knowledgeable about the long-term repercussions of divorce and who will be honest with you (perhaps not always telling you what you want to hear). By counseling restraint, they may save you from yourself.

Read books on divorce and custody issues. Play the odds and follow their advice.

Participate in counseling, if only for a short period of time. At the very least, you may learn ways to help your children through the divorce.

WHEN DIVORCE IS DESTRUCTIVE

While the family law system has made some progress in the past couple of decades, I believe that when we look back on the manner in which we handled divorce in the middle/late twentieth century, we will be appalled.

Certainly, inadequate divorce laws and unethical family law professionals are partially to blame for the problems in divorce, but the fact remains that the destructive excesses of the family law system are primarily driven by out-of-control clients.

Out-of-control clients are the ex-spouses who do not honor their obligation to pay spousal support, who hide financial assets, who try to limit and control the other parent's custody time with the children for selfish reasons, who use distortion, false accusations, and betrayal of marital intimacies against their ex-spouse as a litigation/negotiation tactic, who are motivated by vindictive rage and/or uncontrollable fear.

I've been told that clients often gravitate to attorneys who share similar ethics. This can sometimes create problems—an out-of-control, rageful client collaborating with an unethical attorney is able to careen through the family law system and create a great deal of destruction. And do it perfectly legally.

Regrettably, society has come to accept a casual brutality in divorce as normal.

High-conflict divorce can be like a game of chicken, similar to two cars driving head-on toward each other at high speed. The "loser"—the driver who veers off (i.e., compromises)—is the sane one. The "winner"—the person who is most willing to gamble and sacrifice everything for foolish pride, the driver who does not alter course or compromise—is the one who acts insane.

With this philosophy of winning at all costs, the rageful spouse who is willing to risk everything—including the welfare of the children—can manipulate everyone in the legal system. The family law system sometimes gives such spouses what they want just so they'll go away.

Currently, very little can deter a rageful, out-of-control spouse from filing false accusations and distortions or from punishing or harassing an ex-spouse with legal documents and court appearances.

Perhaps because of concerns about government intrusion into what is regarded as a private matter, the legal system takes a hands-off attitude. It presumes that one or both of the litigants have the legal right to play out this pathology until all emotional and financial resources are exhausted and their lives—along with the lives of their children—are enveloped by anger, hostility, and destruction.

While this legal presumption may be appropriate for other types of litigation, it is not appropriate for families and children.

Society needs to intervene to deter this destructive behavior. While confidential mediation and counseling can be effective, I believe that many high-conflict divorce cases would benefit from close monitoring by a court-appointed "referee" who would act as the judge's eyes and ears into a case. This scrutiny may minimize destructive actions by unethical spouses and attorneys.

Additionally, before starting litigation, couples engaged in high-conflict divorce should be required to go through mediation and counseling with a mediator who is empowered to report to the judge at least on the parties' good-faith participation. Litigation should only be a last resort.

Attorneys are often easy, convenient targets for jokes, disparaging remarks, and blame for flaws in the legal system. While some of this is justly earned, the responsibility for many of the legal system's failings must be laid at the public's feet. The system reflects our values, our ethics, the legislation we have adopted, the degree of attorney/client oversight we have chosen.

However, solutions are not always easy to come by; a problem may be more complicated than it first appears. For instance, part of what motivates attorneys is the need to protect themselves from clients who may sue them, claiming the case was mishandled. To give themselves this protection, attorneys must be able to prove that they acted aggressively and diligently on behalf of their client.

In his book *How to Do Your Own Divorce in California*, Ed Sherman writes:

> An attorney who represents you must go to great lengths to protect himself against later malpractice claims by his own client—you. This means doing things for the attorney's benefit instead of yours. California's leading family law authority advised attorneys either to get clients to waive the attorney's responsibility or else "do the absolute maximum" in every case. Doing the maximum may or may not help you, but it will certainly raise the level of conflict and it will cost plenty.

> The attorney works in our system as a combatant, but that is not what you want for solving personal and family problems. Law schools do not require courses in counseling or communications. They teach aggressive and defensive strategy and how to get advantage in every case. Lawyers are taught to look for problems, not solutions.

Participants in the divorce process often behave in a destructive manner because the family law system offers motivations for them to do so.

For instance, by being rooted in an adversarial civil-law tradition, the family law system rewards the litigant who aggressively goes on the attack. Doing so usually gives the attacker a strategic advantage by placing the other litigant on the defensive.

Furthermore, attorneys have little motivation to settle cases; they are rewarded financially for *not* settling. We are relying on the goodwill and personal ethics of an overwhelmed and largely unmonitored legal community to act in a manner that benefits our society around the issue of divorce.

Often, false allegations are made. Too many unethical negotiations take place behind closed doors. Some attorneys can irresponsibly escalate divorce conflict by their single-minded commitment to "getting the best deal" for their client without considering the long-term repercussions for all the parties involved—especially the children.

Child custody disputes, distorted or false accusations of child abuse, or endangerment and unwarranted restraining orders are too often a legal tactic, not a solution for promoting better cooperative joint-parenting.

I'm deeply concerned by the repeated pattern in divorce stories I hear that resonate with: "Even though my ex-spouse has never abused me, I filed for a court restraining order against him/her because my attorney told me to" or "My attorney said I had to stick it to my ex before he/she stuck it to me" or "I filed for sole custody of the children because my attorney said I might not get joint custody if I didn't." The latter strategy is an example of using children as negotiating currency.

Words such as "abusive," "harassing," "neglectful" are used routinely and irresponsibly—often without any consequences for the falsely accusing client or attorney. This is the sort of thing that inflames fear in the separating spouses and that escalates the conflict.

Sometimes, when the false allegations are made often enough, the judge gives them some credence in a final decision—even without proof actually having been offered in court. In other words, the lie becomes the truth.

Success is too often defined as one parent "winning" and the other "losing" custody of the children. We must redefine success in family law as both parents being as equally involved with their children as possible.

For those who are less-than-stellar examples of parenthood, perhaps we should consider mandatory parenting classes or take other steps that promote the bonding of parent and child instead of taking actions that make that bonding more difficult.

I have read about programs that train inner-city youth how to be involved parents. In most cases, these young people were not raised by involved parents and therefore have no role models to follow. Perhaps the family law system can provide similar programs to keep parents involved in their children's lives, even if it requires a long-term effort. Surely the investment made to strengthen parenting and prevent problems for children of divorce when they are young would be less expensive than having to fix problems when the child has matured and been negatively impacted by divorce.

I believe the family law system needs a thorough examination to articulate the professional, personal, and financial motivations for all participants in the procedure—litigants, attorneys, judges, mental health professionals, accountants—and to clearly define and mandate ways to motivate them to perform in a manner that will resolve conflict, not inflame it.

For instance, making a portion of divorce mediation costs tax-deductible might be a motivation for more constructive behavior in divorce.

It's important to note that, while many divorce professionals are well-intentioned, divorce has become a big business. Those who make money in the divorce "industry" may be resistant to change.

Fortunately, progress is being made across the nation as our divorce laws change—but it seems to go at a glacial pace.

PAYING SUPPORT AND LOVING IT

TRUE STORY:

A mom and dad, parents of two young children, decided to divorce. For a few years before the divorce, the mom had been the primary wage-earner, working long hours at the office while the dad stayed at home and raised the children. In fact, a couple of years before, the family had moved to another city to accommodate the mom's career. With the passing of time and the change in geography, this distanced the dad from his former career contacts—it was going to take some time for him to rebuild a career. The judge, being gender-neutral in the ruling, ordered the mom to pay spousal support and child support to the dad. The mom was furious.

The dad was committed to joint custody of the children but wanted the mother to agree to an alternate-weekend custody arrangement (sometimes known as a Standard Freeman Order). This custody arrangement would mean that the children would be at the mom's house every other weekend plus one afternoon or evening per week. (Usually the dad is the parent with less custody time in the alternate-weekend arrangement.) He was concerned that the mom's career prevented her from being available to the children during the workweek. The mother was also furious about this arrangement.

Many in society might view the gender-reversal custody scenario described above as unfair to the mother. Yet in hundreds of divorce agreements and judgments entered into each day, society accepts it as standard if fathers only see their children four or six nights a month.

This story tells us that we are beginning to make small strides toward becoming a more gender-neutral society. It also reveals that (1) not just women consider themselves "gatekeepers" of the other parent's access to children and (2) not just men who react angrily about having to pay support.

Payment of support is one of the most volatile issues for both sides in divorce. For instance:

➤ The primary wage-earner (usually the husband) may feel the amount of spousal support is too large or goes on for too many years. The "out spouse" (usually the wife) may feel that the amount is too small or doesn't go on long enough.

➤ The husband may wonder why the wife doesn't get a job and support herself. The wife may be incensed that her financial partnership in supporting him through college or her hours of unpaid labor as mom and/or house manager are not honored.

➤ It may be galling for the husband to pay support to a wife who dishonored the marriage with adultery or alcoholism. Or the wife may view receiving support as payback for putting up with his adultery or alcoholism.

➤ Support payments can be used as a way of staying connected to an ex-spouse in a negative way. For some people, keeping a negative emotional connection is better than being treated with indifference by their ex-spouse, because indifference leaves them powerless.

➤ The husband may be angry that the wife is using the child-support money for her own comfort (i.e., clothing, gambling, trinkets) rather than for the welfare of the children.

And so the divorce tango goes on and on.

44

I have found some ways to make payment of support relatively pain-less—even to find contentment knowing that the payment of support provides two comfortable homes for my daughter.

First and foremost, depersonalize support payments. Figure out a way to pay (or receive) the money, but minimize its emotional content. Keep in mind that if you had stayed married, the amount you're paying in support would probably have been spent on your ex-spouse and children anyway. Remember that spousal-support payments are tax-deductible to the payer but become taxable income for the recipient.

More spousal-support considerations:

(1) **Paying spousal and child support is mandated by law** and is based primarily on a percentage of the difference in income between the two parties. It doesn't matter whether or not your spouse was an equal partner in the

marriage. Furthermore, marital behavior (i.e., adultery by either spouse) has no bearing on the amount of support. In other words, you chose to be married to your partner for a certain number of years, and whatever the quality of the marriage was, you showed up for it.

Even if your spouse wasn't a full partner, he or she probably made some contributions to your life during the marriage. Acknowledge this and honor it. If you cannot think of any contributions your ex-spouse made to your marriage, you are either excessively demonizing your ex or you made an incredibly stupid choice when you said "I do."

(2) It helped me cope with support payments by categorizing my ex-wife into two entities.

The first entity was as my ex-wife. When I think back on our years together, I am usually able to delineate the good and bad parts of our marriage and focus on the contributions she made to our life.

The second entity was as mother to our children. Each time a woman becomes pregnant, she places herself at risk. My ex-wife did this and contributed to the raising of our children. She was a partner in caring for our son as he died. Finally, while I strongly disagree with parts of my ex-wife's parenting, I know that on those days when my daughter lives at my ex-wife's house, she is adequately cared for. I focus on honoring these qualities in my ex-wife.

(3) It may help to envision spousal support as a business investment gone bad or as a long-term tax or commission payment. Just let it go.

(4) **Support payments may help ensure that your children have two comfortable homes in which to live.**

(5) **Spousal-support payments may be viewed as the price of freedom.** Compare the pain of paying support to the pain of continuing to cohabitate with your ex. With this perspective, support payments may seem like a bargain.

(6) **In most cases, spousal-support payments will diminish or cease** as the years go by or when your ex-spouse remarries, and child-support payments will end when the child is emancipated (usually by late teens or early twenties, depending on state law). You will probably recover financially within five or ten years after the divorce is finalized. True, in some long-term marriages, spousal-support payments can last for the lifetime of the out spouse—almost always the wife—unless she remarries. But in this era of women earning competitive salaries, that legal presumption is diminishing. Again, using a gender-reversal litmus test, it's difficult to imagine society, or a judge, accepting the scenario of a career woman having to pay lifetime support to an ex-husband who stayed home to care for the children.

(7) One woman I spoke with categorized **support payments as a form of child protection.** She had known some divorced wives who unwisely rushed into another marriage seeking financial security. Some of these second (or third or fourth) marriages exposed the children to unhealthy, abusive living environments with unappealing stepfamilies. As my friend stated it, "If a woman is finan-

cially secure, it's less likely she'll marry some idiot for his money and have the children end up with a creep for a stepfather."

Additionally, some research indicates that children of divorce who are raised in two homes by the divorced, not-remarried parents do better emotionally than those raised in blended families with the added stresses of half-siblings, stepsiblings and stepparents.

(8) **If an ex-wife is financially solvent as a result of support payments, the court may require her to pay the lion's share of her own attorney fees.** When she realizes that she is spending her money on the litigation instead of operating under the assumption the ex-husband is paying for both sets of attorneys' fees, the litigation may settle down considerably and be limited to genuine issues rather than manufactured ones.

47

I recently read that in thirty percent of families where both spouses work, the woman's salary is larger than the man's. When I've talked to dads who stay at home and raise the children, I've learned that they become more aware of—and more compassionate about—the challenges and stresses of being the nonsalaried home manager and of having to ask for money from the female wage-earner. Conversely, when I talk with women who are the family wage-earners, I hear them becoming more aware of the challenges and stresses of providing for the financial needs of the family, of being troubled by the manner in which the male partner spends the money they've worked so hard to earn. Now that so many people are experiencing gender-reversal roles in family and career, it will be interesting to read and hear the ensuing societal dialogue in the future. My hope is that we will become a more gender-neutral society in both spousal-support and child custody arrangements.

EMOTIONAL VIOLENCE IN DIVORCE

The child abuse that goes on in divorce situations is one of the biggest unrecognized child abuses. I've seen cases where the mother makes a child get on the phone to the father and say, "Because you're not sending more money, I can't see you anymore."

— from an article in the *Los Angeles Times* quoting clinical psychologist Bruce Derman

EMOTIONAL VIOLENCE

While the family law system is beginning to deal more effectively with acts of physical violence, not enough is being done to define acts of emotional violence, recognize their seriousness, and make parents accountable for them—especially around child custody issues and false allegations in divorce proceedings.

Much of what happens in high-conflict divorce has negative repercussions for decades in the lives of the children and the divorcing spouses. I believe that this long-term impact—often resulting from actions that were carried out with malicious intent—qualifies as emotional violence.

I have also heard the terms "emotional terrorism" and "emotional rape" used in the context of high-conflict divorce.

Emotional violence is hard to pin down. While it doesn't leave visible marks on the victims the way physical abuse does, it is still extremely damaging. The legal system is imperfect enough when dealing with hard, cold facts; it functions even less well with a murky issue such as emotional violence.

The emotional violence wrought by a rageful spouse is an abusive pathology that must be acknowledged and addressed with intervention and close scrutiny by the courts—just as the courts intervene with drug abuse, alcohol abuse, and physical abuse that do harm to others, especially to children.

While mandatory counseling programs and co-parenting classes for litigants in high-conflict divorce exist in some cities and states, there aren't enough of these programs, and they do not function on a long-term basis.

If only a fraction of the money now spent on divorce litigation fees were used instead for mandatory classes and counseling in cooperative joint-parenting and anger management, divorcing couples and their children would be richer emotionally and financially.

Below are some examples of emotional violence in divorce (all of which are discussed in more detail in other chapters):

(1) **Distorting facts or lying about an ex-spouse in legal documents.**

(2) **Betraying marital intimacies an ex-spouse shared in times of trust and using them as a weapon in litigation to satisfy the accuser's rage.**

(3) **Falsely accusing an ex-spouse of physical abuse, sexual abuse, or sexual improprieties.** If this is done in connection with child custody issues, it is an act of emotional violence not only against the adult, but also against the child, who is being used as a tool to express the adult's rage. It taints the child's being, even if he or she never learns about it.

(4) **Making negative remarks (or withholding positive remarks) about the other parent in an attempt to turn a child against that parent.** This is an act of emotional

violence against both the child and the parent. (See "Brain-washing Children," page 62.)

(5) Manipulating a child in order to validate a parent's feelings about him/herself. For instance, the custodial parent may limit the child's access to the other parent, perhaps in the hope that enforcing dependency in this way will make the child ignore the custodial parent's flaws. The goal: to make an adult feel good at the child's expense.

(6) Refusing to communicate or cooperate with the other parent or minimizing the existence of the other parent. Doing this places the adult's need for privacy ahead of the child's need for cooperative joint-parenting.

(7) Allowing a child to witness acts of physical or criminal violence by adults, especially by parents. This carries such severe emotional consequences that some people believe it should be criminalized—that anyone who commits a criminal act in the presence of a child should be charged with the additional crime of emotional violence against a minor. I understand that prosecuting such cases may not always be practical, but I believe it's an important philosophical statement for our laws to make.

55

Emotional violence against others is an act of violence against one's own soul.

THE MANUFACTURED VICTIM

When a couple divorces under highly conflictive circumstances, both parties often expend a great deal of energy portraying themselves as the victim. Each can become emotionally invested in doing this.

Some attorneys can inflame this perception, seeing it as their job to "manufacture" a victim out of their client to gain advantage in negotiation or litigation. However, the existence of a victim requires the existence of unfair—or abusive—treatment by another party: a victimizer. Taking this path in divorce litigation can immediately escalate the conflict—the person who has been labeled a victimizer may not react kindly to this tactic. It can easily lead to retaliatory accusations.

This manufacturing of a victimizer can originate from the accusing spouse or his/her unethical attorney or both. For instance, the soon-to-be-ex-spouse who is a moderate social drinker may now be characterized in legal documents as a full-blown, neglectful, abusive alcoholic who is a danger to spouse and children.

Once the finger-pointing and name-calling begin in court documents, a line is crossed that can do long-term damage to any cooperation between the ex-spouses. Making accusations must only be done in cases of genuine abuse.

While many states have officially adopted "no-fault" divorce with the intent of deescalating divorce and steering the system away from blame and accusation, "fault" divorce still lives on in manufactured victimization.

No doubt those who work within the family law system hear of and witness genuine abuse to a degree I cannot imagine. I do not want to diminish the existence of real victims in society. But when a client and an attorney manufacture a victim—for the purpose of gaining advantage in negotiation or in court judgment—they dishonor the real victims.

This litigation strategy is, in fact, an additional act of violence against genuine victims, for it pulls the limited resources of the family law system away from the real victims who truly need assistance.

Because of the existence of real abuse victims (especially when the allegations involve children), judges may understandably err on the side of caution. This can result in a subtle assumption of guilt against the accused rather than the assumption of innocence by which we are all supposed to be protected. Ironically, this can create a whole new category of genuine victims: the falsely accused.

Once an allegation or implication of child abuse or endangerment is made, that child's world is tainted: Parents, teachers, doctors, friends, and relatives become cautious and wary.

It is possible to set up one's own victimization. For instance, one parent may chase off the other parent with litigation to acquire sole custody of the children, then revel in the sympathetic role of being the abandoned single parent who is tired, overwhelmed, and victimized by the non-involvement of the other parent.

57

The motivation to manufacture victims should be neutralized. This is an area where closer scrutiny of client and attorney behavior may provide a deterrent.

BETRAYAL OF INTIMACY

We are intimate with another person when we share our inner self. We "open up" by lowering the protective shields to our soul and making ourselves emotionally vulnerable.

When we share intimacies, we entrust another person with our most private—and not always most pristine—thoughts and actions. None of us is free of imperfect thoughts and deeds. Each of us is an easy litigation target if we trust the wrong person with intimacy.

At best, sharing intimacies brings people closer to one another. At worst, making ourselves emotionally vulnerable by sharing our souls hands the listener a lot of power—and the potential for that power to be abused.

High-conflict divorce is often an ugly war of betrayal of intimacy. It is two former allies, like friendly nations that once shared military secrets, who are now enemies that are trying to destroy each other using the intimate knowledge acquired in times of trust and partnership.

Intimacy is a thing of great value and deserves the utmost respect. Yet in the family law system it becomes a weapon, a weapon that is used too often and too callously.

How you handle and respect the issue of marital intimacy is a test of your ethics. You may not get encouragement from your attorney or from the family law system (which often rewards betrayal of marital intimacies) to act with restraint.

Often in high-conflict divorce, one or both litigants will put on an air of concern or fear and claim that they were compelled to betray marital intimacies in legal documents for the purpose of protecting themselves, protecting the children, or even protecting the ex-spouse from self-inflicted harm. (The latter tactic can give the accuser the enormous emotional power of being both saintly savior and executioner.)

This can be another example of manufactured victimization and is an act of emotional violence.

The people we honor as most moral are those who do not betray intimacies under even the greatest duress: journalists who go to jail rather than reveal sources, captive soldiers who will give up their lives before revealing their comrades' position to the enemy.

Acting morally means allowing confidential information to be revealed only under a certain set of specific, tightly defined circumstances that indicate genuine danger to a person. In other words, we must hew to the same guidelines followed by priests, mental health professionals, and doctors.

My understanding is that such professionals, even when they see thousands of "clients" in a career (many of them married couples whose relationship is in trouble), feel compelled to report abuse in only a very small percentage of their cases. Yet in family law, "discovering" abuse and filing restraining orders seem to be routine occurrences. I am concerned that family law attorneys and their clients seem to "discover" so many dangerous or mentally ill people in the opposing camp.

Miraculously, ex-spouses who have been accused of being mentally unstable and/or dangerous are often "cured" through attorney negotiations. That is, the "charges are dropped" if the accused will give up a certain amount of custody time with the children or pay the ex-spouse a certain amount of money. In other words, it was never a mental health issue but a negotiating tactic.

This is an abuse of the mental health profession. Regrettably, the family law system has little or no accountability for this. I also wonder why more objections aren't registered by the mental health community.

Perhaps part of the answer to this lies in the fact that the mental health community also reaps financial benefits in the divorce industry; a certain partnership exists between attorneys and mental health professionals who specialize in divorce. An attorney will usually be able to find a mental health professional—a paid expert witness or "hired gun"—who will conform to the attorney's view of the case.

Betraying intimacies may result in retaliation by the accused spouse/attorney team, who, following the philosophy that the best defense is a good offense, return fire with their own betrayals and distortions of marital intimacies. Inevitably, the result is escalation of the conflict. When this happens, the only guaranteed winners are those with billable hours: the attorneys.

Betraying intimacy and making false or distorted accusations with the intent to harm is an act of emotional violence. For many people who are victims of such experiences in the family law system, the inner struggle to trust or be intimate again with another person can be monumental.

If you are a victim of this type of abuse, the best thing you can do for yourself and for the world is to say "yes" to life by working toward retaining your capacity for trust and intimacy in future relationships. Doing so may take a lot of effort. But if you never trust again, if you never risk entering another relationship, if you lose hope, you lose the essence of life. When this happens, malice wins.

BRAINWASHING CHILDREN

A child is being brainwashed when one parent does or says something in an attempt to undermine the child's relationship with the other parent.

Brainwashing children can be subtle (one parent minimizing the existence of the other by erasing any reference to him/her in conversation or photos) or overt ("Your father doesn't love you—he doesn't send me enough money to take care of you!").

Brainwashing is sending the child a message that says, in effect: "You and I are allies against the world. We are best buddies. I wish you didn't have to be with that other parent, but there's nothing I can do about it—you and I are victims of a system that wrenches you away from me three days a week and that forces me to share you with the other parent. Someday you'll be old enough to choose where you want to live, and I just know you'll choose my house."

Brainwashing or programming children is usually done to convince the child that one parent is better and more loving than the other. Parents who excessively demonize the ex-spouse want their viewpoint to be validated by others—especially by the children. If they can sway the children to "vote" for them, it validates them as the good person and the ex-spouse as the bad person.

A 1991 study of 700 families titled *Children Held Hostage: Dealing with Programmed and Brainwashed Children* (Clawar and Rivlin, American Bar Association, 1991) reported that brainwashing and programming occurred at least occasionally in eighty percent of families. The study found that some level of brainwashing and programming occurred more than once a week in fifty percent of families and, in the families who were experiencing high-conflict divorces, brainwashing and programming commonly occurred more than once a day.

In the book *Healing Hearts*, author Elizabeth Hickey writes:

> According to the Clawar and Rivlin study, women are often the worst offenders. Bitter mothers represent the majority of likely programmers. The study contends that women have a sense of ownership of their children and a conditioned view of their role. Also, women are overwhelmingly "awarded" custody of their children and thus spend more time with their children.
>
> Remember that once upon a time you, too, could see the good in the child's other parent. Your child now stands at that point.
>
> What is best for [children] is a healthy relationship with both parents, and they need permission from each parent to enjoy a relationship with the other.

Brainwashing can result in severe, long-term emotional damage to children. It distorts their perception of reality. For instance, they may perceive Mom as a good parent, but that doesn't coincide with what they hear Dad saying about her. This can result in children doubting their own sense of reality, having low self-esteem, withdrawing from relationships, becoming mistrustful or misinterpreting the world around them—in extreme form, all symptoms of paranoia.

Brainwashing children may backfire against the parent who does it. When children grow up and learn the truth about both parents, learn that they have been lied to and used as a tool for one parent's vindictiveness, they sometimes limit or sever contact with that parent.

In extreme form, the programming of children is known as "parental alienation" (PA) and "parental alienation syndrome" (PAS). In the book *Divorce Casualties*, Douglas Darnell defines the difference between the two:

> Parental alienation focuses on how the alienating parent behaves toward the children and the targeted parent. Parental-alienation syndrome symptoms describe the child's behaviors and attitudes toward the targeted parent after the child has been effectively programmed and severely alienated from the targeted parent.

Excessive brainwashing or parental alienation may result in a court cutting back or terminating child custody for the offending parent.

Some examples of brainwashing:

"WHEN YOU COME 'HOME' FROM YOUR 'VISIT'"

Many parents say something like the following to their children as they drop them off at the other residence: "When you come 'home' from your 'visit' at Mom's house, we'll do something fun." This implies that one residence and parent is primary while the other residence and parent are secondary. In certain circumstances, it can even imply that time spent at the primary residence is "fun" while time at the other residence is not.

On days when the child is in your care and goes off to school or to a friend's house, it's okay to use the term "home": "When you come home from school, we'll go to the park for a while." But if it is a transition day to the other parent's house, use neutral phrases: "When you come back to my house on Saturday, we'll . . ." or "When I pick you up from your mom's house on Saturday, we'll . . ."

It's best for the child if parents treat the two residences as equally important, not portraying one as primary and the other as secondary. I hope the term "visit" will someday disappear from divorce vocabulary altogether.

SABOTAGING JOINT CUSTODY

Sabotaging joint custody is doing things that make the child's transition to the other parent more difficult. It can be tearfully saying goodbye when the child leaves your care, thereby making the child reluctant to leave. It can be keeping the child up late watching television or having sleepovers (where not much sleeping is accomplished) on the night before a transition to the other home. This usually results in the child being cranky, tired, and out of sorts at the other parent's home. If this happens often enough, the child may begin to associate the other parent's home with being cranky and tired—and may grow reluctant to go there. The best script to follow is, "You must go to bed on time tonight. You're going to Mom's/Dad's house tomorrow, and you need to be well-rested because you're going to be doing lots of fun stuff over there."

It's important that children know you will be fine without them, and it's vital that they spend quality time with both parents. Each parent must honor the child's custody time with the other parent by behaving in ways that make transitions as easy as possible for all concerned.

65

MAKING NEGATIVE REMARKS ABOUT THE OTHER PARENT

Making negative remarks in an attempt to turn a child against the other parent is an act of emotional violence against both the child and the other parent.

A parent is part of a child's soul. When destructive, negative, critical remarks are made about a parent, it damages a part of the child's soul—you are sending the message that you despise part of the child. The same is true when the source of those remarks is a relative or family friend.

Think back to when you were still in love with your ex; try to recall how much it hurt or angered you when others said unkind or insulting things about your spouse. Or think about how it feels when someone makes derogatory remarks about your family, your race, your religion, your ancestral culture, your political views, your city, your former school or college, your favorite sports team.

When a child hears ugly things said by one parent about the other, it hurts deeply. As adults, we have the choice of responding to an insult by making a retort or by walking away. But children aren't yet prepared to do this. They have no choice but to listen to the hurtful remarks, sometimes year after year.

WITHHOLDING POSITIVE REMARKS ABOUT THE OTHER PARENT

Withholding positive remarks about the other parent is also destructive, in a passive-aggressive way. It is a subtle way of encouraging the child to favor one parent over the other. Manipulating a child in this manner is an act of emotional violence.

The best thing we can do for our children is to find ways to say positive things about the other parent. Sometimes this may be extremely difficult, but doing it is an act of love for the child. It makes the child's feelings our primary concern.

These positive statements about the other parent may be small ones ("Your mom/dad was a good tennis player in high school"), but they must be truthful.

When children have regular access to both parents, they learn the truth about both parents. Insecure parents may want to limit a child's access to the other parent, fearing that they will not compare well in the child's eyes. When parents manipulate a child to validate their own feelings about themselves, they harm the child, who has no real choice and becomes an emotional hostage.

REFUSING TO COMMUNICATE OR COOPERATE WITH THE OTHER PARENT

Refusing to communicate or cooperate with the other parent or minimizing the existence of the other parent places the adult's selfish wishes ahead of the child's need for cooperative joint-parenting.

It can also be a way of sabotaging joint custody. For instance, Mom may have made plans for hosting a play date or dinner party following a weekend transition from Dad's home. If the child has a bad cold and is unable to socialize, and Dad (who knew about the social engagement) purposely withholds this information from Mom until the moment of transition, he creates a scenario that will heighten the parents' conflict. He has sabotaged the occasion by withholding information that would have allowed the other parent to make alternate plans.

Another tactic some parents use is to withhold information about school activities, music or dance recitals, sports activities, doctor and dental appointments, medication instructions, and so on.

Some of this may be contrived to make the other parent look and feel foolish or to convince the court that the other parent isn't involved in the child's life. ("He shouldn't be awarded joint custody—he doesn't even know about our child's medication needs!") But it may also be done to plant seeds of doubt in the child's mind, with the hope that he/she may think something like, "Gee, if Dad doesn't know about my school stuff, he must not care as much as Mom" or "If Dad says Mom doesn't give me my medicine correctly, I'm safer at Dad's house. He cares more."

KEEPING SECRETS

Yet another level of abuse occurs when the child is asked, perhaps in unspoken ways, to keep secrets from the other parent. The child is manipulated into being a co-conspirator in the withholding of information.

Children must not be burdened with the responsibility for keeping secrets about one home from the other parent. Such communication is often subtle—for instance, a dad may introduce his new girlfriend to the children and say, "Don't tell your mom about this. It'll make her mad, and she'll make a scene." Not only does he tell them to keep a secret, but he is portraying the mom as angry and vengeful, planting doubt and fear in their minds about the mom.

Or consider a case where a dad finds that his ex-wife has been involved in a lesbian live-in relationship for a year. The dad doesn't mind that the mom has a new lover, doesn't even mind that the relationship is homosexual, but does mind that the children were told about it a year earlier and have been brainwashed to keep it a secret.

A good rule: Whatever you tell your children about important issues in your life, you must tell the other parent.

You may justify noncommunication with the other parent by thinking, "I've never told the children they can't talk about events or people at my house. If they don't feel comfortable enough or close enough to the other parent to discuss things freely, it's another indication that I'm the parent they like the best." This isn't true. Children need permission from each parent to speak freely about their life at the other household. You give this permission by communicating openly with the other parent about important events and people in your household—and making sure the children know you've done this, so they feel safe to express themselves freely in both homes.

Whether overtly or by an unspoken understanding, whenever you give your children the message, "Don't tell Mom/Dad about this," you are damaging them by putting them in the middle of your conflict with your ex-spouse.

For an excellent, comprehensive discussion of brainwashing, see Chapter 3 of *Healing Hearts* by Elizabeth Hickey and Elizabeth Dalton.

DEMONIZING YOUR EX

Our brains are structured in such a way that, as we enter into a relationship, we can become intoxicated with love, blinded by love.

In fact, when we become sexually aroused by another person, our brain undergoes an intoxicating chemical change that inhibits our ability to reason. Our judgment is quite literally impaired—Mother Nature doesn't want us mulling over biological consequences as we enter into romantic encounters.

This doesn't just occur with a brief romantic encounter. Accurate judgment about another person can be impaired by romance for weeks, months, or years. (Remember how you couldn't understand the negative reactions of friends and family when you chose inappropriate people to date?)

Human beings enjoy the feeling of being intoxicated—whether it's a child spinning in the yard until he gets dizzy, an adult experiencing a religious/spiritual euphoria, using alcohol or drugs, or the heady, breathless excitement of romantic love.

As we enter a relationship, this romantic intoxication can cause us to ignore or downplay our partner's failings and quirks. This is a necessary bit of delusional/distorted thinking; without it, we wouldn't make the plunge into marriage.

As we exit a relationship, we often need to do the opposite: ignore or downplay our ex-partner's good characteristics and magnify the bad ones. This is also a necessary bit of delusional/distorted thinking, enabling us to make the break out of marriage.

This is demonizing the ex-spouse.

Demonizing your ex is a natural reaction in divorce, and, when done to a moderate degree, is probably a necessary emotional purging. Demonizing your ex can also be a way to create a protective barrier against the possibility of reconciling and reentering the relationship. But this purging/demonizing can become extreme and destructive.

At the beginning of a divorce (and perhaps forever after), you may find it sheer torture to be in the presence of the person who, years ago, you had pledged to love, honor, and respect for the rest of your life. The personal characteristics that your ex-partner has probably always possessed—many of which you were attracted to at one time—have become intolerable.

For instance, the man you once admired for being ambitious in his career is now regarded as controlling and obsessive—or the woman who you once admired for being spunky is now regarded as bitchy and crazy.

You may now hate your ex-spouse. You may refer to him/her with obscenities. You may wish misfortune to plague his/her personal and business life (perhaps thinking that if your ex-spouse's life falls apart, it can validate your probably mistaken, childlike belief that he is nothing without you or that you were indispensable to her existence). You may even wish your ex were dead.

I believe that excessive demonizing of an ex-partner is a delusional type of mental illness. It becomes a serious situation when it evolves into what I refer to as "rageful spouse syndrome" (see page 75) and becomes the fuel that allows divorce cases to spin out of control.

Excessive demonizing of your ex can be especially problematic when you enter litigation and retain an attorney. When you meet with your attorney and plan how to approach the case, he/she will try to filter through the facts as you present them to get an accurate picture of the situation. Be fair with your assessment of your ex-spouse; get reality checks from friends and therapists about the accuracy of your perception. This will best serve your interests—if you begin litigation with inflammatory misperceptions and false accusations, you (and your children) may pay a high emotional and financial price for many years.

An attorney can easily plan a case around your distorted perceptions of your ex-spouse, to go aggressively on the attack, to help you play out your personal rage in court.

This approach is also safer for attorneys, because if they've covered all the legal bases, the risk of your making a future case against them for inadequate representation diminishes.

Furthermore, a rageful spouse is an attorney's dream—he/she can be the source of a steady stream of fees.

The courageous, ethical attorney filters through the demonizing of your ex and recommends restraint. He/she knows that the best thing for you is to move forward in your new single life and to have a long-term, civil, cooperative co-parenting relationship with your ex-spouse.

Demonizing your ex may also be an attempt to garner sympathy from friends, family, therapists, attorneys, and the judge. Portraying yourself as the victim can be a seductive life role.

A victim never has to acknowledge playing any part in the breakup of the marriage. It is much easier to say "He/she was abusive" or "He/she was crazy." Being the victim diverts attention from your own negative personal characteristics or behavior.

It's amusing to hear of couples who, when married, were co-conspirators in minor financial shenanigans—doing a little cheating on income taxes, "liberating" items from a place of employment—but who suddenly become righteous during divorce proceedings. One will express surprise at what a crook the other is, claiming to have no knowledge of the family financial irregularities or swearing to have participated out of fear.

People who excessively demonize the ex-spouse may need their perception to be validated by others. They enjoy hearing friends and family spout negative things about the ex; they enjoy seeing the ex skewered in attorney letters and legal documents. They believe the ultimate validation of their perception is a favorable court ruling, and they will go to great lengths to achieve this.

It can be infuriating, even devastating, if other people don't share their perception. So much energy, time, and litigation—all dedicated to proving what an evil person the ex-partner is—have been wasted!

Excessive demonizing can be a perverse way of staying connected to an ex-spouse. If you hate your ex, you are still emotionally tied to the marriage. You'll be emotionally divorced only when you feel indifferent, hopefully even civil, toward your ex-spouse. Perhaps the best you'll be able to muster is a feeling of discomfort, something like the feeling you might have for a slimy relative with whom you must socialize on family holidays.

You may need to fake civility around your ex-spouse for the sake of your children. Doing so places your children's needs before your own.

Don't waste your life energy on negative, vengeful thoughts and actions. Move forward in positive ways. Honor the good parts of the relationship that existed at one time. Honor the emotional needs of the children involved.

Also remember that the relationship existed in part—fifty percent, to be exact—because of your choice. You showed up for it.

"RAGEFUL SPOUSE SYNDROME"

I am not a psychologist or psychiatrist, nor do I have any academic cre-
dentials that entitle me to formally categorize anything as a "syndrome."
However, I believe a label for the out-of-control litigant in the family
law system is long overdue. Somebody has to step up to the plate and
take a swing at the issue, so for now it'll have to be me.

In the book *Mom's House, Dad's House*, Isolina Ricci refers to the people
who fuel prolonged, high-conflict divorce litigation as "hostility junk-
ies." Whatever you call them, they create an all-too-common pattern in
divorce cases, and one that the family law system and legislators do not
adequately address.

I have chosen the term "rageful spouse syndrome" to describe what
I consider a form of (sometimes temporary) mental illness. I believe
this rageful condition is a pathology and hope it will someday be officially acknowledged by mental health professionals, attorneys, and judges
in the family law system.

Rageful spouses can manipulate everyone involved in the divorce;
they are willing to sacrifice everything and everyone around them to
act out their rage. They feed on being victims. They can hold other
participants hostage with their anger and can exact extraordinary compromises. People are cautious around rage and its unpredictability. Few

onlookers, including a rageful client's attorney, will confront this rage head-on.

In many cases, rageful spouses have experienced physical and/or emotional abuse at some period in their life. Years of bottled-up rage can be directed at a wrong—but convenient—target: the ex-spouse. This is why I believe high-conflict divorce is in large part a mental health issue, not a legal issue.

Some of the symptoms I believe exist in a rageful spouse:

➤ Without a prior pattern or record of abusive behavior by the ex-spouse, rageful spouses are quick to file for restraining orders, make false accusations of sexual or physical abuse, make false accusations of drug or alcohol abuse, and so on to gain strategic advantage in litigation or negotiation.

Sometimes worse than false accusations are distortions in court papers or letters between attorneys. Implying, shading, and distorting are common when no actual proof of wrongdoing exists; litigant and attorney attempt to sow seeds of doubt in the judge's mind about the opponent's character. Because distortion contains the foundation of real events or facts, it may be more difficult to defend against than out-and-out lies.

➤ Rageful spouses will not voluntarily enter into long-term mediation or counseling to resolve differences. They erect an impenetrable shield of attorneys and accountants around themselves and stay on the attack, using lies and distortions as a mainstay of their arsenal.

➤ They will not cooperate or communicate with the other parent in joint parenting or will sabotage a joint-parenting arrangement in passive or aggressive ways. These are parents who place their rage or their need for privacy ahead of their children's need for cooperative joint parenting.

➤ The rageful spouse engages in legal dirty tricks and uses the court system as a weapon to "get even" or to "teach my ex a lesson."

➤ Rageful spouses may change attorneys several times because they cannot find an attorney who will be aggressive or punishing enough toward their ex. I have heard of a case in which an ex-spouse kept divorce and post-divorce litigation active for years by hiring and firing a series of fifteen different attorneys.

➤ They excessively demonize the ex-spouse, even to the point of being delusional.

➤ They engage in prolonged or chronic litigation, which can be a veiled form of stalking and harassment. The word "compromise" is not in their vocabulary.

➤ Rageful spouses will spend $10,000 in litigation fees to acquire $1,000 from the ex-spouse, whether it is rightfully their share or not. They are willing to sacrifice their children's college fund or inheritance, retirement funds, or a house down-payment to validate their rage through litigation.

➤ They are spiritually weak, self-centered people whose need for a feeling of power is satisfied by the drama of litigation. It fulfills them to see attorneys, accountants, and the opposing litigant react to their provocations. The rageful spouse feeds on, is addicted to, the conflict and drama that depletes most of us.

The mental health of rageful litigants is compromised when, intoxicated by anger or fear, they lose sight of reality. As M. Scott Peck writes in his book *The People of the Lie*,

> Mental health requires that the human will submit itself to something higher than itself. To function decently in this world, we must submit ourselves to some principle that takes precedence over what we might want at any given moment. For the religious, this principle is God, and so they will say, "Thy will, not mine, be done." But if they are sane, even the nonreligious submit themselves, whether they know it or not, to some "higher power"—be it truth or love, the needs of others, or the demands of reality. As I defined it in *The Road Less Traveled*, "Mental health is an ongoing process of dedication to reality at all costs."

The mentally healthy person acknowledges his or her negative behavior, perhaps apologizes for it, but certainly attempts to curtail it. In contrast, rageful spouses are fearful, narcissistic, mentally unhealthy people who are unable to acknowledge the reality of their negative behavior and need to find a scapegoat for the turmoil in their life. Lacking healthy shame, they continue to engage in negative behavior.

Closer monitoring of high-conflict divorce cases may help to keep this rageful behavior under control. Monitoring may also serve to protect the rageful spouse's attorney from unwarranted lawsuits alleging mishandling of a case.

As a friend of mine put it, part of the problem in dealing with a rageful ex is that "we mistakenly look for logic from a crazy person."

PART III

THE PLAYERS

I spent a dispiriting year in court trying to prove my fitness as a father. It was a time when I met a series of reptilian lawyers so unscrupulous that I would not have used their marrow to feed wild dogs or their wiry flesh to bait a crab pot.

— from the novel *Beach Music* by Pat Conroy

THE PLAYERS

The "players" in the family law system:

➤ **litigants**

➤ **attorneys**

➤ **judges**

➤ **mental health professionals**

➤ **mediators**

➤ **accountants**

➤ **paralegals**

➤ **secretaries**

➤ **court clerks**

If a child custody evaluation is done, the testimony and observations of doctors, teachers, and friends of the family will also become part of the process.

It is highly likely—pretty much a guarantee, in fact—that some or all of these people will make mistakes and errors in judgment during the process.

The more people you have involved in your divorce, the greater the likelihood of errors. As decisions about your children and your finances are made by others, you begin to lose control of your destiny.

Some of the errors in these decisions may be devastating—especially concerning child custody. Appealing or modifying custody rulings is usually difficult and expensive.

Mediation, counseling, and direct communication with your ex-spouse limit the number of people involved, which can substantially minimize errors.

At this point in your life, you need things to go smoothly. If you choose to proceed in a litigious manner, other people's errors will exacerbate the mistrust, tension, and hostility between you and your spouse.

When important issues are being decided about your finances and your children, you want a great amount of care and deliberation taken about your particular situation. The people who can do that best are you and your ex-spouse.

84

The primary players in the family law system are attorneys and mental health professionals (either of whom may also be mediators).

It's important to know that these two professions are composed of people whose approaches to conflict-resolution may be fundamentally different. According to attorney Forrest Mosten in a March 25, 1997, article in the *Los Angeles Times*, the reason more cases do not go to mediation has to do with the way lawyers are educated, with an emphasis on competitive one-upmanship instead of preventative, healing models: "The word 'client' is never used in law school, and the word 'apology' does not exist in the legal language. We study cases, not people."

While the attorneys and mental health professionals often work together, there seems to be an underlying struggle between them for the philosophical heart and soul of the family law system.

Attorneys can be wary of including mental health professionals in a case because:

➤ they know that the more people involved, the more unpredictable the outcome;

➤ the unethical attorney may be wary of the scrutiny of mental health professionals;

➤ some less-experienced mental health professionals can make errors or be in over their heads when dealing with couples in high-conflict divorce;

➤ there are limits to what even an experienced mental health professional can accomplish with some litigants in high-conflict divorce;

➤ mental health professionals are often hired by attorneys as expert witnesses, so their perception and testimony might possibly be influenced by future employment opportunities in the family law community.

However, most mental health professionals are committed to de-escalating the conflict and do not engage in inflammatory finger-pointing or accusations—which are the tools of some attorneys. Because of this, I believe society would be better served if mediators and mental health professionals played a larger role in the divorce process, especially in the early stages.

If you are in a high-conflict divorce, especially if it's a child custody dispute, think about consulting with a mental health professional experienced in divorce proceedings in addition to working with your attorney.

Child custody issues and financial issues can become unethically mingled, one being used as leverage against the other for negotiation. Even though child-support payments are sometimes based in part on the amount of time the child spends in each home, custody issues and financial issues should be kept separate as much as possible.

Be prepared for occasional conflicting advice from various disciplines. And be aware that, in most cases, the judgment and philosophy of the attorney will prevail. The family law system, as currently designed, is ultimately a legal arena.

Remember the following:

➤ attorneys are trained to deal with contracts and negotiations

➤ accountants are trained to deal with financial matters

➤ mental health professionals are trained to deal with emotional matters

If either you or your estranged spouse have these professionals working on issues outside of their training and experience, your divorce will probably be a mess.

MENTAL HEALTH PROFESSIONALS

Conflict between divorcing spouses needs to be managed and minimized. If conflict escalates out of control and engulfs the divorcing spouses and their children, healing and the forward progress in life cannot begin for any of the family members. Very often, mental health professionals are effective in managing emotional conflicts between divorcing spouses.

Mental health professionals may play several roles in the divorce process.

MEDIATORS

When mental health professionals function as mediators, they will most likely address child custody issues—such as helping the divorcing spouses work out a shared-parenting plan. However, if both ex-spouses can maintain a constructive working relationship, these same mental health professionals may also help them resolve financial and property disagreements. In such a case, agreements made in mediation should be reviewed by each spouse's attorney before final acceptance.

CO-PARENTING COUNSELORS

In this capacity, the mental health professional works to steer divorcing couples away from their individual feelings of anger and hurt and instead focus them on the needs of their children. Such a counselor tries to sensitize the adults to the children's view of the divorce. Very often, divorcing parents are so caught up in their grief and anger that they aren't emotionally available for their children; they fail to notice and take care of their children's grief and anger about the divorce.

In co-parenting counseling, issues of shared parenting may be worked out. Additionally, divorcing couples learn

➤ to keep anger in check so it doesn't become a destructive force;

➤ to redefine their individual boundaries as single people and find emotional closure in the reality of their marriage's end;

➤ to redefine their parenting relationship, remaining partners in raising their children while avoiding inappropriate contact and unnecessary litigation;

➤ to find new ways to communicate with each other about their children's needs;

➤ to communicate with their children about the divorce;

➤ to be sensitive to the emotions their children may experience about the divorce—such as grief, anger, confusion, shame, and so on;

➤ to keep their adult conflicts and emotional needs from encroaching on their children's lives;

➤ to distinguish between normal, less-than-stellar parenting and genuine child abuse or endangerment. (It is important to note that an ex-spouse's concerns about child abuse sometimes are not based in reality, but are the product of the demonization of his or her former marriage partner.)

INDIVIDUAL THERAPIST FOR EITHER OR BOTH OF THE DIVORCING SPOUSES

When undergoing individual therapy, a divorcing adult may learn about many of the issues mentioned directly above. In addition, individual therapy often addresses issues of grief, because divorce involves emotionally processing many losses: the loss of marriage, the loss of a sense of family, financial loss, the loss of social standing in community, the loss of residence for one or both spouses, and so on.

COURT-ORDERED EVALUATORS

In a child custody evaluation, a mental health professional is assigned (or stipulated by mutual agreement of the divorcing parties) to assess the family situation, to recommend a shared-parenting plan to the judge, or to determine if one or both parents are unfit to care for their children.

Many mental health professionals who perform evaluations of separated families try to do more than merely recommend a child custody time-sharing plan. They also may work with the court, divorcing spouses, therapists, and attorneys to help the children maintain full relationships with each parent and to steer the parents toward some form of cooperation based around the lives of their children.

In the event that a child custody evaluation takes place, each spouse may retain the services of a mental health professional who performs family psychological evaluations in other cases for the court. Such an individual will advise and prepare the parent for the evaluation process. This is not cheating, but a way of educating the parent about the process so he or she may present his or her viewpoint accurately to the actual court-appointed evaluator.

89

SPECIAL MASTERS

Nolo's *Pocket Guide to Family Law* defines a "master" or "special master" as "a court-appointed official who helps the court carry out a variety of special tasks in a specified case. For example, the master may take testimony or permit discovery of evidence. She then prepares a report for the judge. In many family law proceedings, some routine matters, such as uncontested divorces, are conducted by a master."

The responsibilities of a master vary from state to state. They may even have limited judicial powers to act as a "tie breaker" when divorcing parents have minor disagreements about child custody.

In California, a special master may only be assigned to a divorce case if both parties agree to it. However, in some states, the court may appoint a special master without the agreement of the divorcing parties.

CHILD THERAPIST

Therapists can help children work through the upheavals divorce brings to their lives and learn how to set personal limits and boundaries that will keep them free of their parents' conflicts.

It is important that children of divorce—especially those caught in the crossfire of high-conflict divorces—participate in therapy. Children need a safe zone in which to express and explore their feelings about divorce. A therapist can provide this emotional sanctuary. If the parents are in conflict and not cooperating, neither parent can provide a truly safe, neutral environment. Children know that anything they say to either parent may be misconstrued and may escalate the conflict.

A FEW BASICS ABOUT ATTORNEYS

It is your attorney's job to ensure that you get a fair shake in the divorce process. Part of that job is being skeptical, suspicious, and mistrustful of the other spouse and opposing counsel. However, an unethical attorney can use this to justify "milking" or "churning" a case to keep it alive unnecessarily.

For instance, every small mistake made during the divorce can be seized upon by an unethical attorney or accountant, magnified, and waved around as evidence that the client is a victim and the ex-spouse is a victimizer. This escalates the conflict, which means more involvement by everyone, which probably means more errors. The result is that you and your family get sucked into the legal vortex.

Another wrinkle in this litigation drama is that the attorney you have hired to "get" your ex-spouse now knows you as a litigious person, so the attorney will undertake self-protective measures. This can mean he/she will begin blaming the other side for any errors or misunderstandings. Such finger-pointing also heightens the conflict and generates paperwork meant to deflect future litigation.

In all fairness, it should be noted that attorneys must push the limits of the law—their doing so often helps society better define legal and moral standards. Many of our legal and safety protections (due process, limits on search and seizure, automobile and tobacco regulations, and so on) are a direct result of litigation.

Yet we need to impress upon family law attorneys (and clients) that pushing the limits of procedural propriety under the guise of getting the best deal for the client may not, in fact, serve that client well in the long run—especially if one considers the children's needs for a cooperative relationship between their parents.

The divorce laws themselves—especially concerning financial matters—are pretty fair and clear-cut. It's in misinterpreting, distorting, and pushing the boundaries of these laws that clients, attorneys, and accountants cause problems.

I've spoken to dozens of people who have gone through divorce, and frustration with attorneys and the family law system is a common complaint. What I've never heard from a divorced person: "When my ex-spouse and I divorced, our attorneys did a great job. They met with us and, as a team, they:

> informed us about the most likely scenarios for support payments and division of assets based on the law and prior court rulings;

> educated us about the benefits of cooperative, communicative joint parenting and said they were committed to it for our children's sake;

> described the destruction a high-conflict divorce can cause and counseled us to avoid it;

> assured us that they would do their utmost to minimize and equalize our emotional and financial losses;

> ➤ vowed not to engage in name-calling, finger-pointing, or inflammatory tactics;

> ➤ acknowledged that misunderstandings and errors would be made, but that their job was to de-escalate them with good-faith communication;

> ➤ were committed to long-term mediation by a neutral third party before engaging in litigation."

The fact that this scenario seems so absurd is troubling. It shows that we have accepted current family law practice, even though virtually everyone I have ever spoken with believes that this system does not serve the public well.

Divorce professionals are a close-knit bunch. In many communities, attorneys, judges, accountants, and mental health professionals work together or oppose each other year after year, attend conferences, co-write divorce or custody articles, attend the same functions.

This "good ol' boy/good ol' girl" network may seem incestuous and lacking in oversight, and to an extent it probably is. However, when the legal system is working at its best, these relationships result in fair compromises and reasonable settlements. The bottom line is that you want your attorney and your ex-spouse's attorney to have a cordial, constructive working relationship.

ATTORNEYS: ETHICAL VS. UNETHICAL

Attorneys are like the rest of us—there are heroes and villains. As with most other issues in life, this is not a simplistic black-and-white one; many attorneys are a complex mix of the traits mentioned below. Furthermore, one person's unethical attorney may be another person's zealous advocate. In any event, the ethics of the attorney you choose can have a deep, long-lasting impact on your life and the lives of those close to you. Here is a simplified list of traits to look out for.

ETHICAL ATTORNEYS

I've been told that the most important distinction between ethical and unethical attorneys is that an ethical attorney will tell you the unpleasant truth of a situation instead of telling you what you want to hear. It takes courage to be an ethical attorney because, by not taking the most aggressive course, he/she may be vulnerable to accusations of mishandling a case. It's easier and more lucrative for an unethical attorney to generate large amounts of paperwork to validate your demonization of your ex.

In general, an ethical attorney will counsel restraint throughout the divorce process. He/she knows that divorce is a volatile time and that the conflict with your soon-to-be-ex-spouse will, in most cases, eventually settle down. The ethical attorney will discourage you from attacking your estranged spouse with lies and distortions in legal paperwork, for he/she knows that your and your childrens interests are best served by a cooperative relationship with your ex-spouse.

An ethical attorney will work to keep you, opposing counsel, and the judge focused on the law and how the law applies to your case, steering all participants away from the shrill, self-indulgent accusations that are often a part of the family law process. For instance, it doesn't matter if you or your ex-spouse committed adultery. The law doesn't take that into account when spousal-support payments are calculated, so mentioning it in attorney letters or court documents serves only to escalate hostilities.

The attorney will concentrate on keeping the negotiations businesslike rather than indulging in mudslinging or exaggerating financial or custody claims in the hope that the judge will "cut the baby in half." In the long run, it serves you best if your attorney is ethical and has credibility in the divorce community—the judge is more likely to give such an attorney the benefit of the doubt on issues where evidence is not clear-cut.

As part of his commitment to resolving the conflict, the ethical attorney will be the one who tells you to compromise on certain issues so you can move forward in your life. He will try to filter through a client's demonizing accusations to find the truth about the ex-spouse so that the case is based on reality, not vindictiveness.

UNETHICAL ATTORNEYS

Unethical attorneys take advantage of human misery. They use tactics that throw gasoline on the fire. They posture; they inflame a situation by writing letters filled with recriminations against an ex-spouse; they use dirty tricks to rattle an ex-spouse; they file court papers filled with distorted accusations against an ex-spouse; they may even laugh or joke with a client about the misery they are inflicting on an ex-spouse.*

The unethical attorney is not really interested in a settlement; he prefers to "milk" or "churn" a case to keep it generating fees. He/she will generate inflammatory letters and court documents that manufacture his client's victimization while accusing the other spouse of escalating the conflict.

The unethical attorney relies on insinuations, not facts. He capitalizes on the mistrust, suspicions, and fears of the litigants. He/she dangles the seductive—and unlikely—possibility that the ex-spouse will be demonized for all the world to see.

The unethical attorney may be your buddy, listen to you pour your heart out about your marriage (with the billing clock running), get you stoked up to crush your ex in court, support your desire to teach your ex a lesson. He may seem to be your salvation, the person who you believe will punish your ex for all the perceived wrongs inflicted upon you.

If you have a good moral center, you don't want to punish or crush anyone. That is not a positive, life-affirming philosophy; it is a philosophy of destruction and a negative way of staying emotionally tied to your ex. Move on. Move forward.

Besides, it's unlikely you will teach your ex a lesson. Human nature being what it is, most people dig in their heels and fight back against an attempt to crush them. The unethical attorney knows this and relies on it—it's good for business. It extends the life of the case.

Remember: Unethical attorneys can only receive a limited amount of blame for their behavior. They wouldn't engage in destructive, unethical tactics if the family law system didn't give them the motivation.

---

*If you share in this laughter, stop and think for a moment: You've become spiritually tied to someone who finds humor in inflicting pain on another person.

Here is a list to help you compare the two types of attorneys:

Unethical Attorneys	Ethical Attorneys
(1) are inclined to be fighters— promote a philosophy of winning/losing (remember that every winner requires a loser).	**(1)** are inclined to be listeners— promote a philosophy of compromise, avoiding conflict whenever possible, accepting loss, moving forward peacefully, building a new life.
(2) advise you to take your ex to court and come out swinging—the "do it to them before they do it to you" approach.	**(2)** advise restraint, discourage attacking your ex, will promote assertiveness rather than aggressiveness.
(3) encourage betrayal of marital intimacies to gain advantage in negotiation and/or litigation.	**(3)** *dis*courage betrayal of marital intimacies.
(4) may encourage "strategizing against your ex" or may counsel a limited release of personal information to the opposing party because that information can be capitalized on by opposing counsel—this will likely increase mistrust and suspicion between you and your ex.	**(4)** *dis*courage "strategizing against your ex," may encourage talking and sharing information with the opposing party to better define common ground and achieve resolution. Sharing information can remove suspicion and mistrust, which are two integral elements of conflict.
(5) may imply they can "get" you custody of your children, that you don't have to co-	**(5)** advise you that your children need both parents, encourage to you to set up a civil,

97

Unethical Attorneys	Ethical Attorneys
parent—even if it is merely a matter of convenience or control, not because the other parent is truly a danger. May advertise or brag about the number of cases in which they have "gotten" full custody of children for their clients. This is their definition of success.	cooperative co-parenting situation.
(6) may say: "Don't worry about the expense. We'll make your ex-spouse pay for your legal bills, too."	**(6)** tell you that litigation is expensive and should be kept as a last resort since you may be responsible for your own legal bills plus a portion of your ex-spouse's.
(7) agree you've been abused and controlled for years, so now is your chance to get even, to feel empowered.	**(7)** remind you that it is not the role of the family law system to "punish" your ex-spouse.
(8) may encourage lies and distortions; may twist facts to try to make the lie become the truth.	**(8)** will not be a party to lies or distortions.
(9) may be inflammatory in legal documents or correspondence or engage in legal dirty tricks.	**(9)** point out that engaging in legal dirty tricks will only result in escalation of conflict.
(10) may manufacture a victim and thus manufacture a victimizer.	**(10)** may try to define errors made by both parties, but generally steer all parties

Unethical Attorneys	Ethical Attorneys
	away from blaming and finger-pointing to get them moving forward to resolution.
(11) tell you what you want to hear.	**(11)** tell you the painful truth.
All of these escalate conflict	**All of these *de*-escalate conflict**
(and maximize litigation fees).	(and minimize litigation fees).
	By doing the above, an ethical attorney will steer you away from a natural inclination to lash out at your ex-spouse and thereby escalate the conflict. In other words, an ethical attorney will try to save you from yourself.
	All of the above are reasons why you want your ex-spouse to retain an ethical attorney.

99

JUDGES

Contrary to what you may be led to believe, the last place you want to be is in a courtroom having your case heard by a judge. The outcome is unpredictable, and it's highly likely that you will be bewildered, disappointed, or unpleasantly surprised by part or all of the judge's ruling.

Once the case goes before a judge, the attorney (and client) begin to lose control of the outcome. This is why the majority of cases (about ninety-six percent*) are settled out of court, often at the eleventh hour in the hallway outside the courtroom.

I did an enormous amount of preparation for my divorce trial; I would estimate that my attorney, my accountant, and I generated 25,000 to 30,000 pages of original documents and photocopies over the course of two years. Because of this preparation, because I had already made many compromises prior to trial, and because I did not make exaggerated claims or demands in court, I received a judgment that I regard as about eighty percent favorable.

Yet those few items in the judgment that I regarded as unfavorable still came as a surprise to me. Opposing counsel and accountant had

---

* In his book *Child Custody Made Simple*, Webster Watnik cites a study called the Stanford Custody Project in which researchers Eleanor Maccoby and Robert Mnooken found that just 4% of divorces went to trial over custody issues, with only 1.4% actually completing a trial.

disseminated such a high volume of misinformation and distortion that refuting it all was hopeless, and some of it trickled down into the judgment. My attorney simply had to pick and choose which issues we would refute, and hope that the judge saw a pattern of misinformation by opposing counsel and accountant. On most issues this worked. However, on a few points the misinformation worked for the other side—in other words, the lie became the truth. This happened even though the case was heard over three and a half days of a private trial by one of the most respected judges in the Los Angeles family law community.

I reiterate: My experience was not unique. Bewilderment about the legal process is a common theme among my friends who also went through divorce litigation.

There are several reasons for this:

(1)   None of us is perfect. Judges make errors, litigants make errors, attorneys make errors.

(2)   Attorneys can only present (and defend) a very small percentage of the facts in a case. Choosing those items that will have the greatest impact on the judge's decision is difficult and involves a lot of second-guessing. It is made more difficult when opposing counsel has thrown dozens of manufactured issues or accusations into the court documents, making it impossible for the judge to examine all the evidence carefully. Some issues simply have to be let go with the hope that the judge will not give them too much credence.

(3)   Perhaps human nature leads us to assume that the truth must be somewhere in the middle. Judges are human.

Unfortunately, this encourages unethical attorneys to exaggerate claims in the hope that, if the judge does indeed cut the baby in half, they will have exaggerated more than opposing counsel did and the ruling will fall more to their side than is fair.

(4)   A judge wants to make a fair ruling about the issues but also wants to make a ruling that will motivate the parties not to pursue further litigation. If one side is given a completely favorable ruling, it may motivate that side to waive the judgment in the other party's face or unfairly wield it as leverage in future disputes. A one-sided judgment also invites an appeal by the losing client and attorney—which means that the case doesn't settle down. This is part of the reason why legal professionals often say, "A good settlement [or judgment] is one in which both parties walk away unhappy."

(5)   As members of a close-knit legal community, judges may be reluctant to hand down a one-sided decision that alienates their colleagues. In the case of a "rent-a-judge" (see below), rulings may be structured so as not to alienate either attorney because of the possibility of losing future employment.

(6)   Judges may have personal gender biases such as assuming that a mother is the primary caretaker and a father is the primary wage-earner with lesser parenting skills. (It's strictly anecdotal, but I've heard from a couple of sources that female judges can be tougher than male judges on women litigants and that they are more likely to make gender-neutral rulings.)

Sometimes judges will not take any action; they send the parties back to the negotiating table to work it out. Although this may be frustrating for the litigants, sometimes it is the wisest decision.

There were two ways to have my case heard by a judge:

The first was trying the case in the courthouse in downtown Los Angeles. However, the earliest available court date was almost a year away. Not only was it emotionally healthy to get the divorce finalized earlier, but the amount of attorney and accountant paperwork that would have been generated in that period was not an attractive prospect.

In addition, we had had a few hearings in the downtown courts, and I was not favorably impressed with the level of scrutiny that the judge was able to give the case. He made recommendations or steered attorneys toward settlements that usually had little to do with the reality of the situation. Sometimes he had not even read the court filings. It was mind-boggling. It gave a whole new meaning to the term "overwhelmed."

The second option was what is called "rent-a-judge." This is where the litigants and their attorneys agree to hire a private judge (at a few hundred dollars per hour) to hear the case in a private conference room or courtroom. The outcome is acknowledged by the parties (and the state) to be as legally binding as a trial in a public courtroom. Private judges are often judges who have retired from the public court system.

The advantages to hiring a private judge: 1) getting the trial over with to save time, money, and emotional energy in the long term; 2) removing your case from the overwhelmed public court system.

I know of a case involving a post-divorce modification of support payments in which one attorney and litigant wanted to retain a private judge to resolve the dispute, but the opposing attorney and litigant refused; they insisted on going through the public court system. As a result, it took weeks for the case to be heard and, over that time, the attorneys and litigants stood in the courthouse hallway for a total of three days waiting to go before the judge. This waiting plus pre-hearing preparation cost each litigant about $12,000 in attorney fees—a total of $24,000 spent before they ever saw the judge. This is what people mean when they say that the family law system has broken down.

ACCOUNTANTS

Divorce has many tax consequences (which can vary widely from state to state). For instance, spousal-support payments may be tax-deductible, while child-support payments are not. Some methods of dividing the marital assets have more tax benefits than others. An experienced family law attorney or mediator should be familiar with most of these issues, but the services of a good accountant—or perhaps one accountant for each litigant, if suspicion about honesty is a concern—are a worthwhile investment.

The divorcing spouses must keep close tabs on the accountants to ensure that they are working at an appropriate level of detail and communicating regularly with each other so that minor misunderstandings or errors don't snowball into huge, expensive problems. If one accountant's work is shoddy and his/her financial figures are substantially different from the other side's numbers, it will heighten the mistrust and suspicion of all parties and probably result in increased litigation costs.

If your financial situation is complicated or if it includes a family business that is community property,* you may need the services of a forensic accountant. This person will go through the family-business

---

*A few states place the property of each marital partner into two categories: "Separate property" generally refers to assets accumulated by each party before marriage or after the date of separation or as gifts received during the marriage (such as an inheritance); each party retains these individually. "Community property" generally refers to assets accumulated in partnership during the marriage; these are divided (usually fifty/fifty) after the date of separation.

finances, the family personal finances, retirement accounts, and such with a fine-tooth comb to determine which items are separate property and which are community property. The forensic accountant will create worksheets that place a value on all assets so that you and your soon-to-be-ex-spouse can divide them.

The accountants and attorneys may be assisted by real-estate appraisers, household-goods appraisers, or other experts. You will, of course, being paying for all of this—and you may not like their conclusions. If they are within five to ten percent of what you believe is fair, contesting their figures may not be worthwhile. Move on, move forward; get this divorce finalized.

Unless you and your soon-to-be-ex trust each other on these matters, I recommend going through this lengthy accounting and appraisal process in a formal manner. It can make things cleaner in the long run by minimizing misunderstandings and negotiations in the future.

However, make the appraisal process as trouble-free as possible. For instance, if the other party has family heirlooms—separate-property items—that you insist on having appraised, it may be interpreted as a hostile gesture and escalate the conflict.

If you are discovered trying to hide financial assets or personal property, you will escalate the conflict. At the beginning of the divorce process, most attorneys will probably assume you're hiding a few assets. Once you prove them right, they will proceed to dig deeper and deeper into your life.

Whenever you or your accountant send documents to anyone involved in the divorce, write a cover letter detailing what it is you are sending and keep copies of the letter and documents carefully filed for future reference. Errors and miscommunications will likely occur during the divorce process, and, unless you have protected yourself, the blame may be laid at your door.

PROFESSIONALISM AND ACCOUNTABILITY

I work in the film and television industry as a music composer. I'm accustomed to being surrounded by a high level of professionalism and attention to detail; I am honored to work with some of the most talented artists and technicians in the world.

Over a nineteen-year career, I calculate that I have worked with my colleagues for approximately 60,000 people-hours. During that time, I can remember only a handful of occasions when a colleague showed up late or was unprepared for work that day.

During my journey through the divorce system, I saw very little that approached this same high level of professionalism. Some of that was the result of ethical, hardworking family law professionals simply being overwhelmed by a divorce system that is broken down, but far too much of what I witnessed was professional sloppiness and lack of good-faith communication. This was true not only in my own case, but in other divorce cases being heard in the courtroom. On many of these occasions I remember thinking something like, Thank God these people aren't airline pilots!

Being "professional" doesn't mean never making mistakes, for we all make mistakes. But it means being well-prepared and well-intentioned so that the inevitable mistakes can be quickly overcome.

The divorce system has very little accountability for sloppiness or work done in bad faith. Those who bear the negative impact are the litigants who end up paying the attorney and accountant bills. You may be led to believe that attorneys and accountants will be held financially accountable for sloppy work, but this is largely hypothetical and unlikely to happen. Consequences are only rarely handed out by judges, and only for the most egregious examples of unethical attorney behavior. In most cities, family law professionals are a close-knit group, so the current system may be akin to the fox guarding the henhouse.

The divorce community in any city comprises a surprisingly small group of people who must cooperate on many cases; they cannot afford to alienate their colleagues by holding them accountable when they see unprofessional conduct. In fact, asking them to do so may be asking too much. It could be argued that the long-term interests of the public are best served when these divorce professionals are working cooperatively, not policing one another. Yet most people with whom I've spoken believe that the current family law system is not healthy, and a solution seems elusive.

For instance, I understand that it is common in the Los Angeles court system for civil suits for amounts as low as $25,000 to be heard by a full jury over several days of testimony. Yet divorce actions involving disputes over attorney/accountant fees of $100,000 or $200,000 generated over years of litigation may be fortunate to get only an hour or two in front of a single—usually overwhelmed—judge. This is a legal system that's out of balance. With this system's lack of scrutiny, family law attorneys and accountants have no motivation to check their own excesses.

Attorneys may tell you that there are solutions to unethical professional behavior, such as litigating against unethical divorce professionals or reporting them to the state bar association. But the client may not achieve satisfaction by taking these steps. Additionally, should a divorce litigant believe he/she has been wronged by opposing attorneys or accountants, there is no legal recourse because they were employed by the other spouse.

Litigants who are burned by the shoddy work of family law professionals have little recourse other than to keep extremely accurate records, financial and otherwise, and to mediate and reach an early settlement with their spouse.

PART IV

THE PROCESS

From an article about a high-profile child custody dispute involving two prominent Los Angeles politicians:

This ugly dispute, like many, has been noisy in a way that private affairs ought never be. It has been mean and contentious in a way that decisions affecting the lives of children ought never be.

The process of resolving such disputes, the court system, is maladroit. It steers things off track, so much so that a "good" outcome is no longer possible. The well is poisoned. Too much pain has passed. The best that is left would be an end less bad than all the others.

— Terry McDermott, *Los Angeles Times,* January 15, 1999

THE EASY DIVORCE

Even the most amicable divorce can be complicated, but you can minimize complications through communication and/or mediation.

An easy, amicable, "uncontested" divorce requires trust and cooperation between the parties. However, at the end of many marriages, these two items are probably in very short supply.

You will need to face the reality that dissolving the business details of your partnership in marriage will take time and effort. Add to this the emotional content of divorce and child-custody arrangements, and you may be faced with one of the most challenging periods of your life.

You will also need to face the reality that, especially if you brought children into the world together, you probably will be tied to your ex-spouse for many years—perhaps for the rest of your life.

Constructing your marriage involved legal paperwork (marriage license, bank accounts, investments, retirement plans, social-security payments, house and property ownership, various insurance policies, wills, family trusts, and so on), and dissolving the marriage will inevitably involve more paperwork.

While all of the above documents took years to accumulate, the divorce process makes it necessary to undo them in a much shorter period of time. This can feel overwhelming, both emotionally and from the standpoint of time and energy. Even in the best of divorces, it can literally feel as though the life you carefully planned and built is crashing down around you.

You will probably need professional legal guidance of some kind, at the very least a mutually acceptable accountant and perhaps a mediator. But remember: The more professionals you involve in your divorce, the more out of control it may be. You must find a balance between getting advice from professionals and making your own choices.

Two musician friends of mine recently divorced after nine years of marriage. They handled the divorce by dividing their belongings, selling their home and dividing the profit, and hiring a paralegal to fill out and file the divorce paperwork. Total cost: $650.

During their separation and divorce, they both experienced the normal feelings of anger, betrayal, blame, and sorrow. However, they were able to go beyond the raw emotions of the moment to choose behavior and communication that served their long-term interests.

Despite three or four painful years as they went through separation, divorce, and healing, they have gradually renewed their friendship and are able to work together in musical ensembles, hike together, and be genuinely happy that each has found a new spouse.

MEDIATION

As Winston Churchill once said, there are certain circumstances in which "jaw, jaw is better than war, war."

Mediation (and litigation) is not about winning, but about trying to minimize your losses. You may not be able to resolve all issues with a mediator, but the more you do, the better. You must enter mediation—and divorce in general—with the knowledge that you will be losing many things dear to you.

You will need to compromise—to "blink" on many issues—no matter the venue in which you play out your divorce. With a mediator, those "blinks" can be small and relatively equal between the parties.

However, with litigation the stakes are raised and emotions run high. As the conflict escalates, each side increasingly regards the struggle as a matter of principle. The battle entrenchments become progressively unyielding, and the "blinks" can become large and painful.

Now you're not just fighting over the furniture, but your personal pride and stubbornness become issues. The emotional investment you've made in demonizing your ex-spouse or portraying yourself as the victim can be at stake.

Virtually all the divorced people I've spoken with years after their divorce was finalized have expressed disbelief when they recall battles in which they fought over what they now realize were insignificant issues. Divorce can make people crazy.

Mediators are often attorneys or mental health professionals. Being neutral, they can cut through the inflammatory posturing, distortions, and finger-pointing and present a divorcing couple with the most likely scenarios for their future regarding child custody and support payments.

While mediators can make errors, I know that my own divorce process settled down considerably on those few occasions when mediation took place. During these periods, my legal fees of $2,000 to $5,000 per month dropped to almost zero and were replaced by mediation fees of $150 to $300 per month.

Those few hours with the mediator often resolved issues that had unnecessarily churned for weeks in the hands of the attorneys and accountants. More important, when communication and cooperation increased even slightly between my ex-wife and me, I noticed a marked increase in my daughter's level of happiness.

Mediation is confidential, and any agreements made in mediation sessions can be altered within a couple of days if, after review, you and your attorney believe changes are necessary.

A mediator can help you and your soon-to-be-ex-spouse create personalized agreements, customized to suit your family's needs, rather than cookie-cutter solutions negotiated by attorneys or ordered by the court.

A good mediator will:

➤ run your financial information through a specialized computer software program to calculate spousal and child-support payments. While various factors unique to your situation may affect the final support payment amounts and may require some negotiating, the computer software will get you into the ballpark. (Be prepared to revisit this issue every two or three

years to determine if significant changes in income call
for adjusting support payments.)

➤ recommend ways to fairly divide assets and debts,
explain the tax consequences of various choices you
can make, and work with your accountant(s) on this.

➤ tell you which co-parenting behaviors will give your
child the best chance to cope with the divorce now
and in future years.

➤ help you set up a child custody schedule with provisions
for alternating major holidays, birthdays, and such.

➤ act as a buffer for the hot issues that can cause either
or both of you to react emotionally.

➤ help you communicate with each other (and your
child) about such issues as school, medical care,
adjustments in custody schedule, dating or remarrying, stepchildren.

➤ help you to find ways to redefine your relationship
with your ex so you and your children benefit over the
long term.

➤ keep you looking forward in life, not allowing either
party to refer to the past. Accusations are not considered constructive in mediation. "That was then, this is
now" must be your mantra. Dealing with anger or grief
about the past is best done in individual counseling.

You may need to compromise until it hurts a lot. You may feel that
your ex-spouse is getting everything and you're getting very little of
what you want. It's highly likely your ex-spouse feels shortchanged too.
Only when you have reached an impasse over a long period of time
should you consider entering litigation.

LITIGATION

I've been told there is an old curse that says, "May you win a lawsuit."

This is a reminder that there is rarely such a thing as winning in litigation, that just being party to a lawsuit is a loss of time, energy, and money that could have been spent on more positive life endeavors.

The price of litigation is emotionally and financially high. It will be costly in ways you can't yet foresee. Litigation is a life-draining process.

When you choose to enter litigation, you are gambling. You put your financial security, emotional health, and co-parenting future at risk. The stress engendered by the process may even jeopardize your physical health.

Sometimes good-faith differences of opinion on issues require a hearing before a judge. However, litigation is too often used as an outlet for rage and vindictiveness.

Once the line is crossed from an uncontested divorce into a contested or litigated divorce, everything changes.

You and your ex-spouse are now adversaries in a lawsuit. This adversarial environment will color all contact you have with your ex-spouse for a very long time, perhaps forever.

An adversarial legal proceeding is easy to get into but can be very difficult to get out of—and emotionally and financially difficult to recover from. It may impact many parts of your life in ways you can't anticipate. For instance, your business acquaintances and future loves may be cautious about becoming involved with you—they know you as someone who has aggressively pursued an ex-partner in litigation, and they may fear becoming your next target.

During the litigation process, the attorneys and accountants are, in theory, trying to discover the facts of the case so that they may enter into settlement negotiations. In reality, they may also be figuring out ways to put a spin on the facts to place their client in an advantageous position. How this is handled is what differentiates an ethical attorney from an unethical one.

Once you enter this adversarial relationship with your ex-spouse, the two of you (with the help of your attorneys) will probably begin strategizing against each other to gain advantage. Strategizing against your ex involves divulging the most personal vulnerable points or betraying marital intimacies to your attorney so that they may be exploited as negotiation or litigation tactics. It is one of the ugliest aspects of the family law system, but the practice continues because the system offers sufficient motivation.

You and your attorney must decide how much of this personal information to release in court documents and filings. Remember, the court papers are public record. Your children have the right to read them someday.

Aware of possible long-term ramifications, an ethical attorney will minimize the release of harmful details about your ex-spouse. However, the unethical attorney may—perhaps in a subtle way—encourage you to capitalize on your ex-spouse's vulnerable areas or betray marital intimacies to gain strategic advantage, then distort these claims in legal documents to manufacture you as a victim.

If you are the spouse who initiates false or distorted accusations, know that it will invite retaliation. You must have very legitimate reasons to make serious accusations in your divorce.

If you have decided to initiate divorce litigation, or you have unwillingly been sucked into the legal vortex by the actions of your spouse, the basic steps outlined in the following pages are what you can expect to encounter. (They will vary from state to state.) While these litigation procedures address financial issues, most of the same steps also apply to child custody litigation.

Meet with your attorney regularly and have him/her educate you step by step about the procedures in your state. If you do not know what to expect, receiving legal documents or court paperwork in the mail can be an unpleasant surprise. When you are in litigation, virtually every piece of legal paperwork may be perceived as potential bad news in one way or another. Anxiety can reach high levels. A good attorney will know this and will try to minimize the fear of the unknown by educating the client.

Educate yourself; play an active, cooperative role in your attorney/ client relationship. However, you may still need to make a leap of faith and let the attorney do the work he was trained to do. I would compare it to a doctor/patient relationship: While you may be able to discuss treatment approaches to a certain degree, it's not a good idea to micromanage by instructing the brain surgeon where and how to make the incision.

For detailed information about the legal terminology and process in divorce, I recommend reading *Child Custody Made Simple* by Webster Watnik, *Nolo's Pocket Guide to Family Law* published by Nolo Press, *Guide to Family Law* published by the American Bar Association, or *Divorce Manual* published by the American Academy of Matrimonial Lawyers.

STEP ONE: FILING A COMPLAINT OR PETITION

One party initiates the proceedings by filing a "complaint" or "petition" with the court. In all future legal documents relating to the divorce, this person will be known as the "Petitioner" and the other spouse as the "Respondent."

This petition defines the disputed issues between the two litigants and asks the court to make temporary, or *pendente lite* (pronounced pen-den-tee lie-tee), orders concerning child custody, spousal and child support, and preliminary division of funds so both parties can pay their bills. There may be a restraining order, or injunctions prohibiting certain actions, for the weeks or months until the litigants reach a settlement or until permanent* orders are issued in the judge's decision after trial.

These temporary orders are usually done "without prejudice," which means that, in theory at least, they will not be considered a foundation for future, more-permanent orders or settlement negotiations. However, be mindful that theory and reality don't always coincide; the status quo may become the foundation for permanent financial and custody arrangements.

123

---

* "Permanent" is a relative term here. Hopefully you and your ex-spouse will be communicating and cooperating in future years so that financial and custody arrangements will evolve to meet the changing needs of the children as they grow older.

For instance, if the temporary orders establish that the children live in one home more than the other during the interim period, the attorneys of the parent with primary custody may drag the case along for several months, then argue that the court should not make the permanent custody arrangement more equal in the final judgment because the children have become accustomed to the "temporary" arrangement.

This can escalate the conflict as litigants try to grab all they can to gain leverage at the beginning of a case—which is why making false allegations for the purpose of gaining strategic advantage can be a seductive option for one or both parties.

If your attorney tells you not to worry about the *pendente lite* orders regarding child custody because they're only temporary, you may want to get a second opinion from another attorney. Do not underestimate the importance of the temporary child custody orders. For one parent to be named "custodial parent" during the first few months of the divorce may not seem like a big deal. When this evolves into a permanent arrangement with generous custody rights to you, it may not be a big deal. But when the custodial parent moves your children across the country, it becomes a very big deal—and there might be nothing you can do to stop it.

In his book *The Father's Emergency Guide to Divorce-Custody Battle,* Robert Seidenberg writes:

> The *pendente lite* hearing could be the most important event in your life for the next twenty years.
>
> The secret is this: There is nothing temporary about this hearing. The agreement or ruling emanating from the *pendente lite* hearing is for all intents and purposes set in stone.

Both parents may be bound by court order or final divorce judgment forbidding either parent to remove the child from the county without notifying the other parent, and instructing each parent not to make derogatory remarks about the other in the presence of the child. In many states these orders are generated automatically with a divorce filing.

STEP TWO: DISCOVERY PHASE

This is where attorneys ask each litigant to provide financial information, bank-account statements, investment statements, income-tax returns, various loan amounts outstanding, car and house value, and so forth. The attorneys are trying to get a picture of the financial situation of both parties so they may begin calculating and negotiating division of marital assets and spousal and child-support payments.

Be open and cooperative with this information, but keep close track of the correspondence with cover letters. ("Enclosed are statements from such-and-such date for bank account #XXX.) Keep copies of all letters and documents you send, and organize them—indexed three-ring binders work well. Organizing will help you and your attorney build a stronger case.

Let all parties know that you are keeping close tabs on all exchanges of information. If the divorce escalates dramatically, one party may be ordered to pay some or all of the other's legal fees if blame for the escalation is laid at that spouse's door. Now is the time to begin protecting yourself against that—or preparing to make others accountable for their mishandling of the divorce process. Assume that it's up to you to provide the scrutiny.

INFORMAL DISCOVERY

This is when the exchange of information and financial documents is done in a relatively open, relaxed, and cooperative atmosphere with phone calls, letters, fax, and mail.

This cooperative atmosphere can suddenly sour and turn hostile, so never become complacent about organizing your case. Keep in mind that you are now in an adversarial situation and there may be a great deal of suspicion and mistrust. Attorneys are all too accustomed to dealing with unethical ex-spouses and unethical opposing attorneys. Their previous negative experiences can color their view of you, no matter how honest and well-intentioned you may be.

Because of this, if you resist producing documents or do it incorrectly, they may react in a hostile, suspicious manner. Resistance or discrepancies in your documents are a signal to an attorney to dig deeper into your life.

When discrepancies or errors originate from the opposing side, an ethical attorney will make a tempered, measured response and try to determine which were inadvertent and which were done in bad faith. Conversely, an unethical attorney will use any discrepancies as justification to begin scapegoating and escalating the case—which, of course, results in an increase in their billing hours.

Resistance or discrepancies will also work against you if the case goes to trial. An opposing attorney can exaggerate minor discrepancies and hold them up to the court as "proof" of a pattern of dishonesty or incompetence on your part, perhaps with the hope that the judge will hold you responsible for a portion of your ex-spouse's attorney fees.

To save time and money and to help you get on with your life, try to keep your divorce from going beyond the informal discovery phase. This may mean ballparking the financial numbers. Both parties must be willing to use round numbers and instruct their attorneys and accountants to communicate regularly and openly.

If your litigation goes beyond the informal discovery phase into a formal discovery phase, you may receive a bit more money or pay out a bit less money, but judging by the cases I know of, the emotional and financial toll may not be worth it.

Unfortunately, divorce litigation doesn't often end at this phase. Many couples, once they have entered the legal arena, need more than just a taste of paperwork and bills from attorneys and accountants before they sit down to communicate, negotiate, and settle. The family law system needs to create more mechanisms that discourage couples from going past the informal discovery phase.

FORMAL DISCOVERY

This is when the exchange of information and financial documents is done in a formal, official forum. Under oath, all parties declare that statements made or information exchanged is true.

Information can take the following forms (examples may be found in the Appendix):

Income and Expense Declaration: A document in which both parties detail their monthly and annual income and expenses. You must account for virtually every dollar spent on haircuts, clothing, home maintenance, utility bills, automobile expenses, and such. Filled out by each litigant, the declarations will be compared in order to help determine support payments. However, these have less bearing than they used to. Today, comparing incomes is the primary factor in determining support payments in many states.

Interrogatories: A set of written questions submitted by opposing counsel for you to answer in writing and with backup documentation. Note that it may take dozens of hours for you to compile a response.

Subpoena: An order instructing a witness to appear at a deposition or for a party involved in litigation to produce documents. Failure to comply can mean being held in contempt of court.

Deposition: An oral examination by the opposing attorney of a litigant or other parties who have knowledge that may pertain to the case—such as your child's baby-sitters, doctors, and teachers. A deposition usually takes place at the office of one of the attorneys. The person being questioned is under oath, and a court reporter is hired to record everything said; this testimony carries the same weight as sworn testimony in a courtroom.

In a deposition, the questioning attorney will probe the deposed person for pertinent information. The other attorney will try to limit the scope òf the questions or defend his client from inappropriate questions. Sometimes this proceeding can get ugly, with the questioning attorney trying to intimidate the deposed person into saying something damaging. It can also get ridiculous. For instance, a friend of mine who owns and operates a small bakery was deposed regarding child support. In the deposition, she was asked by opposing counsel how many dinner rolls she "stole" from the bakery every night for her evening meal.

When testifying in a deposition, lawyers often advise clients to keep their answers short and as broad as possible. ("Yes," "No," "I don't recall exactly," "I cannot recall with accuracy . . . ," "Generally speaking . . . ," "To the best of my knowledge . . .") Don't guess about an answer—you are under oath; what you say becomes part of the court record. Give yourself and your attorney lee-way to define the details later in a manner that gives you greatest advantage. Don't show too much of your hand, for it gives the opposing side time before trial to prepare to discredit you. Be cooperative, but don't give away the farm. Don't try to persuade the opposing attorney to see your side of the issue; remember that he/she is being paid *not* to be persuaded by you.

For more on this, see "Tips on Testifying" on page 131.

And so the discovery process drags on over weeks, months, or years. Very little ever happens quickly in the legal system (although when it does, it can be very stressful). This slow pace can be frustrating; but it can also be beneficial in tempering emotional reactions by the litigants and/or their attorneys. Emotional reactions can lead to poor choices in behavior, which in turn can lead to escalation of the conflict.

However, the slow pace also means litigation bills accumulate as time passes and you remain tied to your estranged spouse. Your life during this period may be under a continual cloud of tension, conflict, anger, sorrow, uncertainty—in general, a very negative emotional stew.

Keep in mind that you and your estranged spouse can stop this at any time by coming to a mutual agreement—a settlement—on any or all issues. The attorneys will write up the settlement agreement per your instructions, the court will stamp "approved," and you're on your way into a new life.

But if you can't reach a settlement, you enter:

STEP THREE: THE TRIAL PHASE

To be perfectly honest, participating in and watching a trial from the front row can be thrilling. Trouble is, it can be the most expensive "pay per view" imaginable. It is especially costly if the price includes a potential lessening of contact with your children.

That said, my divorce trial provided some healing for me; there was a feeling of relief to have my side of the story heard by a judge. For me, having an open forum was like a breath of clean air. The scrutiny provided by a trial meant that misinterpretation or distortion was minimized.

However, a great deal of my success was due to the facts that a competent, careful judge was hearing the case, and I lucked into being represented by an intelligent attorney who is committed to honesty, good ethics, and shared-parenting custody arrangements. From what I have been told about the family law system by friends and acquaintances, I consider myself very fortunate to have emerged as unscathed as I did.

I also like to think that my success was due to my attempts to maintain my personal integrity. I would not have liked to participate in my divorce trial if I'd fudged the truth here and there. While perjury is virtually never prosecuted, if the judge senses that a litigant is shading the truth, many bits and pieces of the judgment may go against that litigant—not enough to be appealed, but enough to send a clear message.

TIPS ON TESTIFYING

➤ If you're on the witness stand in a trial or deposition, be honest. Be honest with information, but also be honest in the clothing you wear (not too fancy, not too grungy), your mannerisms, your respect for the proceedings. Admit and apologize for your mistakes. Don't offer unsolicited information. Keep your answers short, to the point, and devoid of he said/she said whining—the judge has heard enough of that to last him/her many lifetimes.

➤ If you don't understand a question, you may ask to have it read back by the court reporter. If you're not sure about the court proceedings or are not sure how in-depth your answer should be, ask for a short, private consultation with your attorney.

➤ Be familiar with your case so that you can, with reasonable accuracy, refer to actual documents or events and their timing. Your testimony should not sound rehearsed or coached. Do not answer questions instantly; give your attorney time to register an objection, and give yourself time to formulate a concise, correct answer that is not an emotional outburst. Opposing counsel wants you to react emotionally so that you will appear to be unreasonable or volatile. Don't give in to the temptation.

➤ Attorneys use pacing to turn questions to their advantage; do not allow opposing counsel to deter-mine the pace of your answers. For instance, an opposing attorney may ask you a fast-paced series of questions on one subject to get you into their tempo, and then, out of the blue, suddenly switch to a different subject. This may cause you to stumble or seem confused. You may answer without confidence, and this can give the impression that you're not being entirely truthful.

➤ Do not attack or argue with opposing counsel, but do not let them bully you with misinformation or distortions in their questioning. You might politely counter with something like, "I can't answer the question as you have phrased it. It misrepresents the facts."

➤ If opposing counsel asks a particularly stupid, inappropriate, or inflammatory question, pause for a while and let it hang in the air. The people in the room will repeat that question in their minds a few times, and its objectionable nature will become increasingly apparent to all. Doing this will give your attorney time to register an objection and may help you portray yourself as the victim of a bullying attorney.

➤ When you are off the witness stand and are listening to others' testimony, do not react with surprise or smirks or little comments under your breath. Stay "small," barely noticeable. Sit still, sit upright, pay attention.

➤ As you listen to the testimony of other witnesses, you may want to keep discreet notes of items you wish to discuss with your attorney on a recess. You know the facts about your case better than anyone, and you may be able to help your attorney by pointing out discrepancies in the testimony of others.

STEP FOUR: THE RULING

It's highly likely that neither you nor your ex-spouse will be happy with the judge's final ruling. Remember that the legal community defines a good settlement or judgment as one where both parties walk away unhappy.

It's also highly likely that both of you would have been just as happy or unhappy with a mediated settlement months or years earlier. Had you obtained one, you'd have saved a bundle in litigation fees, and your post-divorce healing might be nearly completed.

SUCKED INTO THE LEGAL VORTEX

If you are unlucky enough to be in litigation through no choice of
your own, there's not much you can do about it. It is like experiencing
a serious automobile crash: Your life will tumble out of control, and
you will probably be injured. You can grab the steering wheel and hit
the brakes, but to no avail. You can watch it happening, but you can't
do anything to stop it.

In a high-conflict divorce, you may be damned if you do and damned
if you don't. Your ex-spouse may be completely invested in self-victim-
ization and in demonizing you. No matter what you do, that perception will not change.

Sometimes attorneys get caught up in this emotional maelstrom.
In a March 25, 1997, article by Joseph Hanania in the *Los Angeles Times*,
attorney/mediator Forrest Mosten notes that attorneys are sometimes
"hired guns who play out the family pathology." If your ex-spouse's
attorney cannot or will not keep the situation under control, you're
sunk.

It only takes one litigant to keep a case alive with unreasonable
demands. (Virtually all cases would settle if one litigant would give up
all contact with the children, hand over all financial accounts, the house,
the cars, household furnishings—but this is not reasonable.) A divorce
case will not settle down until both litigants are motivated to compromise and enter into settlements before too much damage is done.

The family law system must create more incentives for divorcing spouses to avoid litigation.

It's small consolation, but attorneys go through their own divorces, and, from the stories I've heard and books I've read, they don't fare any better than the rest of us. For more on this, I recommend *How to Find the Right Divorce Lawyer*, in which attorney Robin Page West recounts her own nightmarish journey through the family law system.

STRATEGY

After her divorce was finalized, a friend of mine described her life at that point to be like a photo of a bombed-out city following World War II. It is the black-and-white image we all know of collapsed buildings and rubble-filled streets—making progress nearly impossible. Like the people in those cities, my friend was now faced with the enormous task of clearing away the rubble, then rebuilding the structures of her new life brick by brick.

A high-conflict, protracted divorce is very similar to a war. With innocents—children—caught in the crossfire, the participants engage each other until one or both sides have exhausted their emotional and financial resources.

And as with wartime foes, divorce litigants usually feel righteous. Both view themselves as models of integrity; they are fighting against evil; God is on their side. When they assume that the judge will validate their perception in his/her decisions, they are usually disappointed.

War is all about strategy.

Once litigant and attorney make the decision to file inflammatory paperwork in court, the hostilities can escalate dramatically. When this line is crossed, it becomes difficult to back away. A war has begun, and strategy may become an unpleasant but unavoidable part of your life.

Thinking of your ex-partner in strategic terms is a particularly ugly element of divorce. Once this happens, it is difficult to undo. Mistrust and suspicion will taint your dealings with your ex-spouse for a long time, perhaps forever. This is not good for you or your children.

Friends and your attorney may tempt you into strategizing against your ex-spouse. While mistrust and suspicion are part and parcel of divorce, the litigants can minimize them with direct communication or mediation.

You may want to retaliate aggressively if you are the first to be attacked in court documents, but in most cases such a strategy is neither necessary nor productive. An aggressive approach is usually about personal anger, not about finding a solution.

The best strategy you can adopt is to be organized and prepared. By cataloging every letter, document, and phone call into three-ring binders with index tabs, you:

➤ send a message to the other side that you are serious and that distortions will be refuted with documentation that a judge may scrutinize (this may keep everyone a little more honest);

➤ send a message to your attorney that you are willing to help with paperwork to ease his/her burden;

➤ send a message to your attorney that you expect a high level of performance;

➤ can help your attorney if he/she needs to refer to information or documents quickly during a trial or deposition;

➤ can help yourself if you are testifying under oath— your preparation and organization will familiarize you with your case details, your credibility will increase

markedly, and opposing counsel will not be able to
intimidate or confuse you easily.

Again, I cannot give legal counsel, but I can share a few pieces of friendly
advice that I believe helped my case somewhat. "Somewhat" is the
operative word here, because if your case is out of control, there's very
little you can do but ride it out.

**Once you notice any hint of your divorce becoming high con-
flict, keep close track of all correspondence with your soon-to-
be-ex-spouse, accountants, and attorneys.**

Do not be aggressive or inflammatory, but make sure everyone knows
that you're keeping a detailed paper trail. While the family law system
has little or no accountability for sloppy work or work done in bad
faith by attorneys and accountants, meticulous records may provide a
limited deterrent.

This paper trail should include a record of your good-faith efforts
to avoid litigation by cooperating with requests for documents and information in a timely manner and your willingness to enter into mediation and counseling.

Even so, do not let your skills at organizing a paper trail of evidence give you a false sense of security. Even when you believe your
evidence is absolutely concrete, with no possibility for distortion or
misinterpretation, you'll find it distorted or misinterpreted. Besides, the
judge may see little or none of it anyway.

Remember that the legal system sometimes frees murderers and
sometimes sends innocent people to prison. I've read an estimate that
ten percent of the prison population is innocent of the crime for which
they were incarcerated. Similarly, I believe about twenty percent of the

final judgment in my case to have been erroneous—and I regard myself as fortunate compared with other stories I've heard about the family law system. You are gambling with these same odds in litigation.

Do not motivate opposing attorneys or accountants to become emotionally involved by lashing out at them. Opposing counsel will be glad to use such an outburst against you. In fact, they may even bait you to react emotionally and say or do something irresponsible.

Opposing counsel will be looking for, even manufacturing, targets to shoot at. Stay small. Give them few targets.

Detach yourself emotionally as much as possible. Forget this part of your life; write it off. Grit your teeth and get through it. Focus on the thirty, forty, or fifty years of happiness and freedom you will have once the divorce is finalized.

When you are asked for documents by the other side, give them up quickly, easily, and without fuss. Some of their requests for documents may be designed to rile you or gauge your level of co-operation; the material may never even be looked at by opposing counsel. Don't reward them with a negative or inflammatory reaction—it may damage your case.

With the exception of documents protected by doctor/client confidentiality or attorney/client confidentiality, opposing counsel has the legal right to ask you to turn over virtually every scrap of paper in your life: personal diary, daily appointment calendar, address book, phone records, credit-card statements. Attorneys and judges search for the areas in which you provide the most resistance—a signal that you may be hiding something.

If you have been dishonest in your past personal or financial behavior, now is one of the times in your life when you may want to consider taking your medicine quickly and moving on with your life.

If you have direct written communication with your soon-to-be-ex-spouse or his/her accountants, relentlessly, tersely—but without rancor—point out errors, distortions, insinuations, and misleading statements made by the opposing side. Keep these communications unemotional, short, businesslike, and limited to one or two sentences. Write them, but don't send them until you've had a day or two to condense, edit, and diminish any inflammatory phrasing or tone.

As you write these letters, keep in mind that a judge may read them someday. Judges are weary of long harangues; their daily existence means being enveloped in a constant "he said/she said" conflict. They want factual answers quickly, preferably in one short sentence.

Write letters and send documents the other side doesn't want the judge to read.

Below are two sample letters. If you were a judge, which would you rather read?

Letter #1:

Dear _____:

I received your request for last year's bank statements. I have given those to you three times before. How can you continue to lose these things? Are you completely incompetent? How many more times must I comply with your harassment—and that's what it is—harassment!

(blah, blah and so on for two more pages)

Yours truly,

or

Letter #2:

Dear _____:

Enclosed are photocopies of the bank statements you requested.

This is the fourth time I have provided these to your office. They were previously provided to you on June 10, August 4, and October 16.

If attorney and accountant fees become an issue at trial, this record of your having misplaced so many documents will be submitted to the court.

Yours truly,

Letter #2 contains no anger but has much more impact.

If you send requested financial documents, underline or circle the pertinent parts so that the attorneys, accountants, and judge can see necessary information at a glance. Many of the issues you deem absolutely crucial to your case will get only that—a glance.

Do not lie or distort. It's morally wrong; you are doing emotional violence to your own soul, and once the judge perceives you as untruthful on one issue, it may color his/her judgment about other facets of your case.

A GLIMPSE INTO THE COURTROOM

During my divorce, the Petitioner (my soon-to-be-ex-wife), the Respondent (me), and our respective attorneys—sometimes with our accountants—met several times at the courthouse in downtown Los Angeles. These meetings concerned a couple of specific issues to be heard by the judge, but most were resolved by last-minute negotiations in the hallway or courthouse conference room.

In professional fees, these courthouse visits cost a total of $800 to $1,000 per hour and usually lasted three or four hours. Added to these costs were the dozens of hours of legal and accounting paperwork prepared beforehand and phone calls between attorneys as attempts were made to reach a settlement.

Much of the time I spent at the courthouse involved waiting in the hallway or courtroom. During these times I witnessed a lot of human conflict unfolding around me. The atmosphere was always one of tension and fear. Particularly sad was watching children being led into or out of the child-services office by social workers as custody cases were being determined. Sad, yet it meant that the children were receiving help, perhaps even being rescued from abusive homes.

Posted on the door of each courtroom (the hallway gives access to several) is the calendar for the day—the list of cases to be heard by the judge that morning. (Afternoons are reserved for testimony in a few unresolved cases, deliberation, documents, and rulings to be written by court staff.) Usually twenty or thirty cases are sifted through by lunch. Most of these are resolved by last-minute agreements worked out in the hallway, conference room, or judge's chambers or are placed on a continuance for another day.

I was dumbfounded by the number of times I witnessed situations where:

> ➤ an attorney simply didn't show up, leaving his client to stand before the judge—and before the estranged spouse, whose attorney was present—and sheepishly say, "I don't know where my attorney is."

> ➤ attorneys filled out the wrong forms, or filled out the right forms incorrectly, forcing the judge (with barely restrained fury) to inform them where to get the correct forms and how to complete them. I wonder if clients still had to pay the attorney bills for hours of incorrect pre-hearing preparation and wasted time in the courthouse.

> ➤ receiving two or three stern warnings that they were about to be cited for contempt.

I can't imagine that such behavior would help a client's case. Yet I saw this sort of thing happen many times. The judge meted out no consequences to these incompetent attorneys, so the incompetence persists.

On the three occasions during my divorce that we actually went before the judge on issues unresolved in the hallway (or in the single manda-

tory mediation session), virtually no rulings were made. On some occasions, it was apparent that the judge hadn't read all the legal paperwork submitted by the attorneys. He seemed to be a hardworking, caring judge—but he mostly seemed to be an overwhelmed judge.

I never lost any of these courtroom hearings, but I always walked
away feeling disappointed in an inefficient, tragic family law system.

On one occasion my estranged wife and I attended a court-appointed
mediation session, and the mediator tried to impose some cookie-cutter child custody arrangements on us. We both knew that these options
were not good for our unique situation and that the judge might impose a similar cookie-cutter arrangement. This motivated us to come
to agreements on most issues.

To reiterate: When important issues are being decided about your
finances and your children, you want a great amount of care and deliberation taken about your particular situation. The people who will probably do that the best are you and your ex-spouse.

A FEW BASICS ABOUT CHILD CUSTODY

For most of human history, children were involved with both parents many hours each day by actively helping with hunting or food gathering, helping at the family-owned store (which was often connected to the family living quarters), or working the farm. The father/child bond was severely diminished by the Industrial Revolution in the mid-nineteenth century. Because of industrialization, fathers left the family for twelve, fourteen, or sixteen hours a day to work in a factory or office. This meant that children did not see their father during the day and, when he returned home at night, he was too exhausted to be available to them. Furthermore, as mankind began to explore and work outside local communities in the eighteenth and nineteenth centuries, fathers who worked as soldiers, sailors, miners, railroad workers, and such, were absent for weeks, months, or years at a time.

The mid-nineteenth century also gave us a new tenet of family law called the "tender years" presumption; it stipulated that the custody of children of divorce would be awarded to their mothers. The "tender years" doctrine was based on the belief that mothers were more important than fathers to children's development. In previous centuries, fathers had nearly always been named custodian of children when the rare divorce occurred. The situation was sometimes so one-sided that, in many of these divorces, the mothers were denied any further contact with their children. The tender-years doctrine swung the pendulum entirely in the other direction. The result was another one-sided custody policy.

Even though this gender-biased presumption that favors mothers has been officially removed from states' divorce codes, it lives on in the thinking of much of society and is reflected in divorce judgments and agreements.

As the tender-years presumption dramatically decreased fathers' involvement with their children, both parents found themselves in a gender trap that confined them to rigid roles. Fortunately, we are now seeing more flexibility in the roles of both women and men. At this point in history, women have the opportunity to gain fulfillment in careers and in earning more-competitive salaries; men have the opportunity to gain fulfillment in being closer to their children. Unfortunately, it doesn't seem that the family law system is reflecting society's changes in gender-neutral custody agreements and gender-neutral support judgments as well as it might.

Child custody can be used as currency to punish an ex-spouse or to give a parent a feeling of power and control.

From *The Custody Revolution* by Richard A. Warshak:

> There are some divorced mothers who would do everything possible to keep their ex-husbands away from the children. Often the motive is to punish the father by denying him access to his children. In some instances, the mother may fear for her children's safety—for example, when the father is likely to abuse or kidnap the children. But in many cases, the divorced woman's own hurt or anger clouds her assessment of her ex-husband's worth to the children.

> Even when a mother favors the father's having contact with
> his children, she may request sole custody in order to regulate
> this contact at her discretion.

Just as some moms do, dads can use a child custody conflict to punish an ex-wife for infidelity or other marital transgressions—perceived or real. Furthermore, either parent can abuse the system by using child custody issues as leverage to raise or lower child-support payments.

It is standard in custody rulings and agreements that, except in the most extreme cases, one parent is not permitted to limit or control the other parent's access to a child and thus use access to the children as a tool for manipulating or punishing the other parent. When one parent is named sole or primary custodian of the children, the access of the other parent is clearly spelled out in mediated agreements and court judgments. If the custodial parent denies access to the children by the noncustodial parent, it is considered contempt of court.

Some moms fear that society will view them as uncaring or inadequate as a woman and mother if they are not primary caretakers of their children, and they will fight tooth and nail to retain that standard of self-worth.

From The Children's Rights Council:

> It is a little-known fact that, according to Census Bureau data,
> there are about two million non-custodial mothers in the U.S.
>
> Mothers often have a worse time of not having custody
> than fathers, according to custody observers, because mothers
> are expected to have custody. When mothers do not have custody, people often think there must be "something wrong"
> with the mother. There is "nothing wrong" with the mother.
> Some mothers voluntarily relinquish custody to pursue educa-

tional or job opportunities. Other mothers lose custody in the "win-lose" battles that prevail in our domestic-relations courts.

When the day comes that America replaces the win-lose situation of custody battles with a "win-win" situation in which a child has frequent and continuing contact with mom, dad, and extended family, "non-custodial mom" (like non-custodial dad) will go the way of the dodo bird, except in cases where more restrictive custody arrangements are needed to protect the child.

CHILD CUSTODY EVALUATION

When divorcing parents are unable to agree on child custody arrangements—especially if one is accusing the other of being an unfit parent—a child custody evaluation may take place to help the judge determine a shared-parenting plan or decide whether one parent should be named custodial parent. The custodial parent is "awarded" primary legal and physical custody of the child. (Here again is that unfortunate terminology referring to a child as an object, a "prize" to be "awarded.") Being named custodial parent can be a seductive option, for it means having complete control over the child's life without needing to consult the other parent.

Not having to consult the other parent about medical issues, haircuts, school, sports activities, vacations may seem an attractive scenario. But it may be about a parent's selfish desire for an uncomplicated, controlled environment; it may not be about the child's need to know that both parents are taking an active interest in his/her life by making important decisions as a team. The most important, long-lasting need children of divorce have is the reassurance that both parents were active and equally involved in their lives. Research shows that a child's self-esteem is directly linked to parental involvement.

As a child custody evaluation begins, parents begin to strategize and collect "evidence" against each other (again, using intimate knowledge of vulnerable points learned during the marriage or gleaned from things said by the child about the other home). One or both parents may coach the child in subtle ways—though this is considered brainwashing a child, and, if a parent is caught doing it, the court may impose severe consequences. The parents often do everything possible to position themselves advantageously for the evaluation.

A mental health professional is retained to evaluate the family situation and make recommendations to help the judge determine a custody situation that will best suit the needs of the child. The evaluator may be selected by the judge and may be on staff in the family law department or child services department of local government. For those litigants who can afford it, a private mental health professional outside the court system may be selected by mutual agreement of the attorneys (pending approval by the judge). This can cost many thousands of dollars.

The evaluation may take several weeks or months. During this time, the evaluator may meet with each parent, meet alone with the child, visit each home to observe the child in the different settings, and interview other adults in the child's life, such as doctors, teachers, and babysitters. (This is known as "interviewing the collaterals" or doing "collateral interviews.")

The evaluator will then write a report that is submitted to the court and to each attorney (who will try to put a spin on it to favor the respective client). All of this can get expensive, further escalate the hostilities, and diminish any hope for a cooperative-parenting arrangement in the future.

The evaluator and judge may note that, at the beginning of the divorce proceedings, one parent suddenly became significantly more interested in spending time with the children—perhaps hoping to have a favorable impact on child-support payments received or paid, or seeking to be named "head of household" (fifty-one percent or more of custody time) for additional income-tax deductions. The evaluator and judge may also determine that the parent seeking sole custody of the child is making false accusations against the other parent (which may result in severe legal consequences for the accuser).

The court may also consider the willingness of each parent to cooperate and communicate around the child. As noted in "Brainwashing Children" on page 62, there is a syndrome called "parental alienation" in which one parent actively tries to sabotage the child's relationship with the other parent. It may backfire and result in the court granting primary or sole custody to the parent who is more willing to foster the child's contact with the other parent. Sometimes referred to as a "nudge from the judge," this is an attempt by the court to motivate the sabotaging parent to behave otherwise in the future.

In many cases, the judge orders a cookie-cutter custody arrangement that neither parent is happy with. The litigants are back to square one; they must restart the negotiation process to modify the court order and create a more realistic arrangement suited to their particular situation.

151

THE CUSTODY GAME

Below are some possible outcomes of a custody evaluation. To estimate your odds of "winning" a custody battle, get a pair of dice, roll once, and compare the result with a number below:

   1: (You can't roll a 1 with a pair of dice.)

   2: The mental health professional who is the evaluator will

draw incorrect conclusions, and the judge's ruling will be based on those errors.

3: The mental health professional who is the evaluator will make an accurate assessment of the situation, but the judge will ignore the report and make a ruling that is not in the best interests of the family.

4: The mental health professional who is the evaluator will make an accurate assessment of the situation, but one of the attorneys will discredit the report, and the judge will make a ruling that is not in the best interests of the family.

5: The judge (who may or may not have followed the evaluator's recommendations) will order some form of joint custody. It will likely be a standard cookie-cutter custody arrangement that leaves all parties unhappy.

6: Ditto #5.

7: Ditto #5.

8: Ditto #5.

9: Ditto #5.

10: Ditto #5.

11: Ditto #5.

12: Ditto #5.

The bottom line is that a custody evaluation is risky. Decisions about your children will be made by family law professionals who may not be attuned to your particular situation or who may make errors—sometimes grave errors—in the process.

You will lose control of important decisions affecting your child. While unpleasant custody orders can be modified if both parties agree, the process can be expensive and time-consuming—and difficult, after any semblance of trust and cooperation between the parents is damaged by the accusations hurled during the initial custody battle.

Divorcing parents have a moral obligation to honor their children by creating a cooperative shared-parenting custody arrangement. You may need to do it through gritted teeth, but, for the sake of your children, do it.

THE CHILDREN

We quarrel, we agree,

We are friendly, we are not friendly . . .

but we have no right to dictate through irresponsible action or narrow-mindedness the future of our children and their children's children.

There has been enough destruction.

— comments made by King Hussein of Jordan about relationships between countries in the Middle East after the signing of the Wye peace agreement in October 1998

CHILDREN FOR SALE

TRUE STORIES:

From a mom's attorney to a dad's attorney:

"If he [the dad] will pay her [the mom] a large sum of money, my client will withdraw her request for sole custody and agree to joint custody of the child."

Overheard from a dad's attorney:

"We're going to surprise the mom and file for sole custody of the children. That should take her mind off money matters."

The children in these stories are human beings who are being treated as property—possessions to be bartered and sold. And, being young, they are unable to voice objections on their own behalf. These children are caught in a family law system that, through lack of close oversight of parents and attorneys (and lack of harsh consequences meted out by the court for unethical behavior), allows this practice to continue.

While the "selling of children" is not always as overt as in the above examples, it is routine negotiating leverage used by unethical parents and attorneys. This is the sort of thing that crosses a moral line in such a horrible way that it can make forgiveness by the other parent—or by the children in future years—very difficult.

The conversations described above took place over phone lines or in court hallway negotiations without witnesses—or they are unspoken understandings between attorneys. Fortunately, the attorney response to the first example was, "We do not buy and sell babies in this law office." But apart from that attorney's personal ethics, there is no oversight or deterrent to this tactic.

These examples explain why I am not confident that attorneys and clients can be trusted to handle divorce without closer oversight by society. These types of negotiations would not take place in an open forum—in front of a video camera, for example. If the participants would not want a custody negotiation to be replayed and scrutinized, there is a high probability that it is unethical.

Fear of losing contact with a child or a desire to punish an ex-spouse by limiting his/her contact with the children can easily seduce some parents into taking the low moral road on this issue. Because the family law system, as currently designed, has few deterrents for engaging in the selling of children, only your own sense of ethics can keep this from happening. If your attorney says something like, "That's how divorce is done—you have to play the game," it may be time to find a new attorney.

"DON'T WORRY, CHILDREN ARE RESILIENT"

While this may be true to an extent, it is one of the most troubling phrases concerning divorce.

Often the phrase "Don't worry, children are resilient" is followed by "I know a child who, fifteen years ago, went through a divorce and turned out fine."

Some even believe that children of divorce have a certain advantage in life by being "toughened" through the experience.

While such things may be said in an attempt to offer reassurance to parents who are concerned about the impact divorce will have on their children, too often these phrases can be used to minimize children's feelings or gloss over poor parental choices, poor attorney choices, poor court decisions/judgments, and poor legislation that are harmful to children.

Stories about the child who "turned out fine" or who was "resilient" fly in the face of statistics, which tell us that children of high-conflict divorce are more likely to:

➤ have difficulty in relationships,

➤ be divorced in adulthood,

➤ suffer depression and other mental health problems,

➤ suffer academically,

➤ engage in criminal behavior and drug or alcohol abuse.

I would not characterize this as "resilient." I would characterize it as "impacted."

Children do not have the coping tools that most adults do of articulating, discussing, and rationalizing the pain, fear, and confusion surrounding divorce. Sometimes the *only* thing young children have are the feelings, which can be overwhelming to them.

It is the adults who must provide—sometimes over and over and over again—the answers and clarification to help children cope with the events exploding around them. Keep in mind that young children need to process emotional difficulties repetitively.

However, if divorcing parents are focused solely on their personal rage and vindictiveness, they will not be able to provide the extra support and coping mechanisms children need to get through the ordeal.

Of my adult friends who were children of divorce, those whose parents communicated and cooperated with each other have adjusted well. By contrast, those whose parents stayed in conflict and hostility or who had one parent absent from their life still carry the pain with them. They have a sad corner of their heart that quickly comes to the surface when we discuss divorce and custody issues.

Adults are often unaware of how vulnerable children can be around emotional trauma. We tend to forget to look at the world through a child's eyes. I highly recommend the book *Put Yourself in Their Shoes*, by Barbara F. Meltz, which helps parents understand this issue.

To illustrate my point, I offer a personal example. A few months ago, after receiving my biweekly allergy shot, I was descending in an elevator at a medical building with an elderly couple. We stopped at the next floor, and a young mother got on the elevator carrying a little girl who looked to be about three—and who was crying vigorously. The mother smiled a bit apologetically at us, pointed to the Band-aid on her daughter's arm, and said, "She just had a vaccination."

The elderly man gently leaned into the little girl's face and said, "There, there. It doesn't hurt." I blinked in bewilderment but refrained from saying, "What do you mean by telling her it doesn't hurt? Of course it hurts!" Predictably, his comment did nothing to diminish the little girl's crying.

Fortunately, the elderly couple exited at the next floor. After the doors closed again, I leaned over to the little girl and said, "I just got a shot in my arm, and mine hurts a bunch. It sounds like yours hurt, too." The little girl stopped crying, sniffled a bit, then told me all about her unpleasant experience in the doctor's office.

The elderly gentlemen wanted to fix her pain and his own discomfort at her crying. But his need for comfort took priority over her need to express her discomfort. His comment was also a distortion of reality; the reality is that injections hurt!

Often what children need most is some sympathy and validation that their pain is real. Validation of feelings is very important to all humans, but especially to children. Not only does it help them emotionally, but it helps them define what's real in life.

CHOOSE ME! CHOOSE ME!

As parents divorce, they can begin a grotesque, emotionally damaging competition of manipulating a child into choosing one parent as the favorite. Usually this is done in subtle, murky ways under the guise of kindness and caring. It's a form of brainwashing.

The manipulation can last beyond the first few months of a divorce. It can sometimes continue for decades.

With young children, this can be about which parent buys more toys and candy; which parent takes the child to more amusement parks; which parent has fewer rules about television, chores, homework, bedtime; which parent is the better "buddy" or "confidante."

Having a child choose one parent over the other can be the ultimate validation for the emotionally troubled parent who wants to perpetuate the victim/victimizer scenario. But using a child to validate one parent's negative feelings about the other is emotionally harmful to the child.

This "choose me" strategy is often done with a long-term view in mind. Parents who have reluctantly entered into a shared-parenting custody arrangement know that, when children of divorce reach their teens, they often choose to live primarily in one home rather than shuttle back and forth between two homes. Both parents can spend years jockeying for affection in hopes of influencing the child's decision when that time comes.

I've been amazed (and disappointed) at the number of times I've heard divorced parents say, "When my child reaches adolescence, I hope he/she will choose to live with me." This kind of comment is usually about the parent's desires or unhealthy needs, not the child's needs. Emotionally healthy parents recognize that they are generating negative thoughts and try to minimize it.

Furthermore, don't forget the maxim, "Be careful what you wish for." I know of a divorced mother who "succeeded" in having the adolescent child choose her house as a primary residence. She discovered that trying to raise an adolescent alone is no picnic.

PART OF MOM, PART OF DAD

The Romans believed that each person has a feminine side (*anima*) and a masculine side (*animus*), and that we need to nurture both parts of the psyche to be healthy. For instance, a person who knows all about sports but nothing about art will not have a balanced life and vice versa. Healthy people and healthy relationships have a balance of feminine and masculine characteristics. We need to experience both in our lives, but especially when we are young and developing our sense of self.

I find that my daughter has many striking (and sometimes disconcerting) similarities to both her mother and me. These traits are not only physical, but also in character—the way she reacts to life, a general life tempo. Perhaps some of these are due to our shared living environment, but I believe most are due to genetic makeup. Her mother and I are literally a part of her.

A famous study done in Minnesota on identical twins who were separated at birth, then reunited decades later, yielded striking results. The researchers found that despite not having contact for decades, many pairs of twins had lived nearly identical lives. Some had purchased cars, houses, and clothing that were identical in style and color, had the same interests, had chosen the same names for their children or even married spouses who had the same name.

But what touched me the most about these studies was that many of the twins said that they had always felt incomplete before the reunion—until they discovered that they had an identical sibling in the world, they always had a nagging feeling that a part of them was missing.

I believe the same is true of children and their parents. Children need to be with both parents regularly. They need to be "at home" with someone who has similar life rhythm and characteristics. Being denied this connection can make a child feel incomplete in many ways.

Perhaps this is one reason why so many adults who were adopted as children go to great lengths to find their biological parents.

This connection is true for extended family as well, which is why I am a proponent of the right of children of divorce to have frequent contact with extended family. After my parents died, I became close to my aunt (my father's sister) and, over the years, found that she and I have a remarkably similar view of life. We share similar sleep patterns, low cholesterol, allergies, sensitivity to our surroundings, sense of nature, sense of humor. To have discovered someone else in the world who experiences the essence of life as I do gives me a foundation. The blood relationship gives me a sense of completeness that I'm not sure can be duplicated with a marriage partner or a close friend.

To cite another example, I have a single-mom friend whose husband left the family when their son and daughter were infants. Now in adolescence, the children are becoming acquainted with their father as he has reentered the picture.

However, before this reconnection took place, my friend would often shake her head, laugh, and say, "When my daughter gets mad at me, she acts just like her father used to! She makes exactly the same gestures with her hands that he used to. She even speaks with similar vocal inflections. How can this be? She's only seen him briefly a few times since she was born!"

Every child knows on an intellectual and spiritual level that he originated from two other human beings. Half of him is from Mom, half from Dad. It is the child's essence, and we must honor that at all times.

Anything said about the other parent is a message to the child about her own being. When one parent says something negative about the other parent, it is a direct message to that child that part of her is flawed, too. We make a moral choice whether to say positive or negative things about the other parent in front of the child.

If you have nothing good to say about the other parent, it may be excessive demonizing on your part. After all, there was a time when you found many positive traits in that other parent (or you wouldn't have engaged in the romantic frolic that produced the offspring).

It may take a lot of hard work on your part, but find good—and truthful—things to say about the other parent. They can be small, but they must be honest. The saw, "If you can't say something nice, then don't say anything at all" doesn't apply here. Ignoring or minimizing the existence of the other parent by saying nothing about him or her is a way of sending a negative message to the child.

The conception of your child was a moment of great beauty in the universe. You must not do or say anything that diminishes or dishonors that.

FOLLOW THE SCRIPT

One of the challenges of divorce is knowing what to say to your children about it as it unfolds over the years. Set the right tone at the beginning, when you break the news to them. Read books on the subject. Get advice from a therapist experienced with children going through divorce.

While parents are usually prepared to answer children's difficult questions about sex and whether or not the tooth fairy is real, the questions and comments children raise about divorce and living in two homes with different routines make the other stuff pale by comparison.

Most importantly, tell the truth (although maybe not the whole truth—children don't need to hear the unpleasant details). Children know when they're being told something that doesn't match what they're experiencing or witnessing. When there are gaps in reality, children use their imagination to fill in those gaps—and they can create dark, damaging scenarios for themselves. ("Mom and Dad are getting a divorce because I'm a bad person.")

If this distortion of reality persists for years, it can permanently damage a child's sense of reality. For instance, having just witnessed a screaming argument between the parents, a child may ask, "Are you mad at each other?" Some parents will actually answer, "No, we're not. Go to bed." If this distortion of reality is a repeated pattern, it can lead to the child misinterpreting and mistrusting everything he/she is told.

Whenever you discuss the divorce with your children (obviously you can say more to older children than younger ones), follow these guidelines:

➤ Tell the truth, but do not assign blame or express anger at the other parent for the divorce. The "script" is to say that you make different choices about lifestyle, and that living together makes everyone unhappy. Words like "different" or "disagree" should be the harshest terms you ever use about the other parent.

➤ If obvious drug or alcohol abuse is involved, take the approach of compassion for your ex-spouse's addiction. Say that, while you hope he/she will recover, you do not wish to live together any longer because it makes you too unhappy and it creates an unhealthy atmosphere for the whole family.

➤ Do not portray yourself as a victim in any manner. This can be a form of brainwashing the children against the other parent.

➤ When in doubt about what or how much to say to your child about the divorce, ask a wise friend (especially an adult who was a child of divorce) or a mental health professional what approach to take.

➤ Imagine yourself discussing these issues with your child while a video camera is recording you and that this imaginary tape will be played someday for friends, family, or perhaps the judge. You'll be amazed how your phrasing will change when you place yourself under this pretend scrutiny.

Or ask yourself, "How would Mr. Rogers say it?" I'm not kidding. It works.

When you tell your children that you are going to divorce (this should be done by both parents together except in the most extreme circumstances), sit your family down and leave your hostility for each other outside the room (Fake it if you have to, but do it—it is a test of your selfishness or selflessness.) Then say the following in your own way:

"Mom and Dad have some sad news we need to tell you about. As you know, we've been fighting a lot, and our home has become an unhappy place. While Mom and Dad loved each other when we were younger, we have become so different that we aren't able to live together anymore, so we're going to live in separate homes to see if that makes us happier.

"Mom [or Dad] will be moving to a new home. You will take turns living with each of us, going back and forth every few days. We'll figure out the schedule soon.

"While our living arrangements will change, the thing that will not change is how much we both love you. We will still be a parent team around you and will both be involved in your life a lot. You are the most important person in our lives.

"The divorce makes us sad, but there will be many good things about it. Each of our homes will be a happier place for us and for you.

"Mom/Dad and I are divorcing because we have too many differences between us. It has nothing to do with you. You are not the reason for our divorce in any way.

"If you have sad feelings about the divorce at any time, tell us and we will listen."

There will probably be many occasions over the years when things do not go smoothly between divorced parents. Keep in mind that intact families have parent tensions as well; it's not just about divorce. But because of the divorce, the level of tension may be very high and it may be necessary to react with a bit more tact and cautious phrasing. For instance:

When your young child's homework or clothing doesn't make it from the other parent's house on a transition day, don't react harshly or blame the parent. Say something like, "It looks like we all forgot to make sure your gym shoes got to my house again. Boy, this is frustrating. Your mom and I will have to find a way to help you keep better track of these things."

When your ex-spouse does something that touches a raw nerve and makes you react emotionally, it's okay to show some frustration. But again, don't blame. Say something like, "Your dad and I disagree on how these things should be handled, and it's frustrating for me. But these disagreements happen in other parts of life, too, such as at school and at work. Many times, when we're dealing with another person, things don't go as smoothly as we want them to."

When your children tell you that they are allowed to watch ten hours of television a day at the other house and they are hoping you will adopt a similar policy, say: "That's one of those things your mom and I disagree on. I know it's difficult for you to have different rules in different homes, but it's something you'll have to live with."

At times, a child may express frustration about a conflict he is having with the other parent. Parents who have a cooperative co-parenting relationship will be able to discuss such issues constructively with each other on occasion. Parents in conflict probably never will. But in either case, the point comes where you can't get involved and may need to say something like, "It sounds like you're frustrated about [such and such] at your dad's house. I'm sorry you're feeling that way. But it's something you and your dad will have to work out between yourselves."

Sometimes children's complaints are genuine; sometimes they are made to manipulate the parents to give in on issues. I've heard of a case where, because the divorced parents were in high conflict and not speaking, the young daughter played them against each other—they were the puppets, she the puppeteer. She enjoyed the power of creating great drama and exacerbating the conflict between the parents. The parents handed her this power by failing to communicate and cooperate with each other.

HELPING CHILDREN COPE

Children's feelings about divorce need to be handled with great care. Their emotional coping mechanisms must be the parents' first priority.

Remember that, as an adult, the years you spent in your marriage represent only a certain percentage of your life. You've had many years living in other family or single situations and have other frames of reference in life to reassure yourself that you'll be able to survive as a single person, or perhaps remarry. You know there is life after marriage. Despite knowing this, divorce may still be emotionally devastating to you.

However, your marriage and family is likely the only existence your children have ever known. It is, literally, their entire world, and now it's crumbling around them. They may feel as though they are in an emotional free fall. They have no other frame of reference in life to reassure themselves; they may not be able to imagine the possibility of a life after divorce. In fact, marriage and family is such a part of their lives that many young children spend years hoping their parents will reconcile. Children may cling to this hope even when the marriage was so bad that they were relieved to see it end.

It would be unusual if your children did not display some emotional effects of the divorce, even signs of depression: crying, lack of concentration, fatigue, emotional withdrawal. The divorce may have a negative impact on their learning, their curiosity about the world.

Below are some basic steps that may assist you in formulating a plan for helping your children through the divorce. I urge you to consult from time to time with a therapist knowledgeable in divorce—especially regarding the best way to break the news to the children, what to expect in their reaction, and how best to handle that in the future.

You may also want to consider having your children see a therapist for a period of time to monitor and minimize their trauma. If nothing else, it's a preventative measure. Having a neutral, safe party to talk to may be very helpful to children of divorce. It's unlikely that either you or your ex-spouse will be neutral enough for your children to feel completely safe to express themselves.

Children commonly blame themselves for the divorce. They often internalize emotions, perhaps thinking they caused the divorce because they misbehaved the week before. Children (and adults who never mature) are egocentric; they view themselves as being at the center of the universe and believe that their actions have great impact on events in the world. You may need to reassure your children that the divorce had nothing to do with them—that it was not their fault in any way, that it was strictly an adult matter between parents.

Above all, do not burden your children with the task of caring for you, of comforting you, of being your buddy to help you get through the divorce. You are here to care for them, with clearly defined parent/child boundaries in place.

GIVE THEM A "SAFE ZONE"

Emotional trauma depletes the resources of our mind and body. Each of us has a limited reserve of these inner resources. When we are taxed trying to cope with trauma, we cannot mature and move forward in life as we do in secure, peaceful times.

To progress in life, most of us need to have some sense of stability—the foundation of a safe zone. When climbing a tall ladder, we need to have a firm grip on one rung before we reach for the next.

Giving children a safe zone so they may begin to heal from the upheaval of divorce is a parent's first priority. A safe zone means stability, peace, mimimal conflict, plenty of cooperation and communication between parents, a continued sense of extended family (keeping grandparent and in-law relationships intact), a predictable routine of shared-parenting custody arrangements, and peaceful custody transitions between parents.

Creating this safe zone begins with the manner in which the divorce is initiated and handled. There is a direct correlation between a child's ability to cope with the divorce and the degree of hostility between parents: The more hostility and litigation, the more damage to the child.

A safe zone also requires that the parent make and enforce well-defined limits on children's behavior, diet, television watching, input regarding their own custody situation, and so on. Children will try to push these limits, but they want you to enforce reasonable rules. It shows you care about them, it shows you are in command and coping, it gives them reassurance.

When adults experience traumas such as natural disasters or auto accidents, we are reassured by the presence of police and firefighters who take control of the situation, tend to our needs, and remove us from a position of having to make too many decisions. Children need this same strength and reassurance from parents.

176

Having this needed strength is difficult when you are emotionally drained from the divorce yourself, or when your children imply that they will love the other parent more if you don't let them stay up late on a school night or don't give them the extra toys and candy that they get at the other parent's home. One of the main reasons you must take care of yourself in mind, body, and spirit is so you will have strong inner resources to be available for your child.

It is best if both parents can agree on similar rules for each house. Moving back and forth between homes is hard enough for children; it is more difficult when those homes have vastly different rules about television watching, bedtime, food choices, and such. Stack the odds on these issues by following the advice of child-development experts. For instance, eight hours of TV per day with a bedtime of 11:00 p.m. is not optimal for a child.

177

VALIDATE THEIR FEELINGS

Let children have their bad feelings; don't talk them out of it or deny that they're hurt. Saying, "You shouldn't feel that way" or "Don't be sad, be happy" is not going to help. Acknowledge their pain and sadness; let them know their feelings are normal. Let them cry for a while. Let them cozy up to you if they need to. Give them comfort.

Don't assume you know what they're feeling. ("I know how you're feeling" is one of the most unproductive things you can say to a sad person.) It's a lot more helpful to say things like, "What are you feeling?" or "It sounds like you're having some unhappy feelings right now. Would you like to talk about what's bothering you?"

Help children build a vocabulary for defining and expressing *their* feelings, not yours. (It's okay to refer to similar emotionally challenging experiences you may have had in your past, but only as a tool for communicating. The primary focus of the conversation must be on the child's feelings.) They will be able to use it throughout their lives as they face other life challenges.

HELP THEM LEARN TO SELF-SOOTHE

After acknowledging and validating their feelings, it's important to teach children constructive ways to self-soothe, to help them learn to create their own healthy safe zones. These coping tools will serve them now and in the future.

Just as adults do, children can use addictive behavior such as overeating, excessive TV-watching, and obsessive shopping to cope with stress. They may be trying to find a safe zone, trying to distract themselves from painful feelings in a predictable, although not always healthy, activity.

Outdoor exercise and activity, connecting and playing games with other people (you, hopefully), art, music, dance, reading: These things that we know are healthy for adults in emotional turmoil are also healthy for children.

It may take years for your child to learn these skills and get past the trauma of the divorce. Be patient and resolute. Seek guidance from friends and counselors. Gently nudge your child into a healthy routine.

HELP THEM DEFINE REALITY AND FIND BALANCE

At some point, the time comes to help guide your child through the raw feelings into the realities of the situation.

For instance, my daughter sometimes got stuck in her sad feelings, cried, and repeatedly expressed her wish that her mom and dad still lived together. On these occasions she would get into a downward emotional spiral, and I had to help her out of it. Sometimes this meant talking her into a more level emotional place by comforting her, validating her feelings, and then helping her to self-soothe. Sometimes it meant distracting her with another activity (yes, even a limited amount of television on occasion).

But I did not invalidate her oft-spoken wish that she lived in one home with an intact family. I listened and acknowledged her feelings. I told her that we all have similar wishes, that her wishes are normal.

You may need to say something like, "I hear you wishing Mom and Dad would get back together so we could be a family again. It sounds like the divorce makes you sad, that it hurts you. I'm glad that you are able to express your feelings so well. But Mom and Dad will never live together again, so we all need to learn to live as happily as we can with this situation. Let's talk about how we might make it easier for you."

That last sentence leads us to the next part. . . .

GIVE THEM SOME CONTROL OF THEIR LIFE

Most of us feel as though our lives are spiraling out of control when a divorce happens—children especially so because they may not be able to comprehend the reasons why their world is crumbling around them. Most people feel comfort when they gain some control of their lives. Give your children some control over changes in their lives—selecting a new paint color for their room, choosing a new lamp. The older the children, the more choices they can handle. These choices must be within *your* acceptable comfort zone (which you will probably have to expand as your child grows older).

I give my daughter (now eight years old) a choice about most things in her life, but I limit the choices to just two or three at a time:

"Yes, it's okay to watch a television show. What show would you like to watch for half an hour: *Arthur*, *The Magic School Bus*, or *Wishbone*?" or "It's time to turn off the television now. Which would you like to do first, homework or practice piano? After you finish those, we can play that game you talked about in the car today. You want to draw instead? Great idea! We'll do that right after you get the homework and piano done."

I try to respect my daughter's individuality in the same manner I would with an adult friend or relative. This means giving her notice of the day's activities so life isn't a series of surprises. It's a matter of extending courtesies such as "We're going to the grocery store in a few minutes. It's time to finish playing. You may bring along a few toys if you'd like to play with them in the car."

Transition days between homes may be a source of stress for a long time, although most children adapt quickly if their parents are cooperating and doing all they can to ease the tension. Disruptions in the custody routine due to holidays, vacations, parent work schedules, or parent or sibling illness may cause emotional turmoil for children, and they will probably not react in the way you wish (i.e., smoothly). No matter which home they're living in on a given day, most children of divorce often miss the other parent.

You will need to be patient and work for years on helping your children cope with the divorce. Acknowledge to yourself, and to them when appropriate, that it will be a part of their lives forever. The divorce and your relationship with the other parent may have an impact on your children's schoolwork, friendships, dating, wedding day, holidays.

Know that you'll make mistakes. Identify them, learn from them, forgive yourself (apologize to your child when necessary), and move forward.

Divorced parents commonly blame their failure in marriage for any problems their children may have. While some instances of behavioral problems, medical, or emotional problems or learning difficulties may be a result of a high-conflict divorce, remember that children who live in intact families have these problems, too.

You may also need to remind your children that parents who are still married also disagree about many issues, such as child-rearing. Tension and conflict exist between all parents, not just divorced ones.

PARENTING

Parenting is the hardest thing I've ever done. It is also the most fulfilling and meaningful thing I've ever done.

Parenting is not occasional visits with a child to whom we are biologically connected; it is being involved in that child's daily life as much as possible.

It is taking a child to and from school, meeting classmates and teachers (so when your child tells you about daily life dramas at school, you'll know the cast of characters), chatting with other parents (I've learned a lot about parenting from other parents), accompanying your child to music lessons, sports practice, doctor appointments.

It is the early morning challenges of waking everyone up at the right time, helping them choose the appropriate clothing (or gritting your teeth and letting your child wear weird clothing on occasion), packing a lunch.

It is the afternoon and evening challenges of making sure homework is completed (and showering a child with praise when it is), piano is practiced, dinner is cooked and cleaned up, television watching is limited, illnesses are cared for.

These challenges and struggles usually provide both parent and child with the payoff of creating a close bond. The times of closeness, peace, and tranquility only come after the challenges have been met and love has been proven. (Sometimes I think children challenge parents to periodically test our commitment to them.)

When we learn how to choose and enforce reasonable expectations and limits on our children, we show them love. They learn about becoming adults as they watch us use our decision-making and coping skills. They also learn valuable lessons when we screw up, especially if we acknowledge our mistakes and apologize when necessary.

They learn about love. They feel loved when they see a parent expending great effort on their behalf, a parent respecting them, honoring them, just being with them.

A close parent/child relationship is created by this multitude of small things. It cannot be phoned in or created by substitutes or formed by participating in a child's life only four days each month. Remember, a child's self-esteem is directly linked to the involvement of both parents.

Regrettably, many parenting plans—most notably the alternating weekend or Standard Freeman Order (one parent being with the child every other weekend plus a short "dinner date" once a week)—do not allow much bonding to take place between parent and child. Bonding is also disrupted when the parents live far apart.

183

Richard Kenyon wrote an article in the May/June 1996 issue of *Yoga International* magazine that is a meditation on the effects his divorce had on his sons:

> I believe my sons are deriving some special, though difficult, gifts from this otherwise undesirable event in their lives. They are getting a crash course in yoga philosophy.
>
> My sons are experiencing some material deprivation that they would not have had with two parents living together. Their needs are met, but their wants are granted—how shall I put

it?—creatively. They are learning that joy does not depend on material things.

They are getting a father who is stronger than he was, or probably would have been, married, and they are getting a father with a clearer sense of his own identity than he probably would have had in the marriage.

My kids are seeing in two households the distinctly different values and belief systems of their parents. Given the chemistry of the marriage, our values and beliefs—or certainly mine—were thinned to a bland soup and could only offer little spiritual nutrition to my children. Now the kids are offered something solid and precise.

Children learn by observing the people around them, especially their parents. Your children will learn from you by observing:

➤ how many different romantic partners you have after divorce, how these partners treat you, and how you treat them;

➤ how you cope with stress and conflict;

➤ how you treat friends and family;

➤ how active you are, your interests in the world—are you a television-watching, junk-food-eating couch potato or are you an active person who embraces and experiences life to the fullest?

➤ how disciplined and focused you are on your work;

➤ how ethical and truthful you are in your day-to-day life. Children learn about hypocrisy when parents lecture them about honesty and then lie about the children's age at a theater box office to save a couple of dollars.

FRIENDLY, BUT NOT "FRIENDS"

You can—and should—be friendly to your young children, but you cannot be their friend. Friendship is based on equality and choice; children have neither in relation to a parent. A child needs child friends, and a parent needs adult friends. These boundaries cannot become muddled.

After divorce, emotionally troubled parents may be afraid of losing a close relationship with a child if they raise their child with structured boundaries, so they stop being a parent and try to become the child's friend. They are afraid that the child will choose to love the other parent more. But a parent must not manipulate a child into a "buddy" relationship by capitalizing on the child's need for acceptance and love. This may fulfill the parent's emotional need for a live-in partner; it does not fulfill the child's emotional need for a parent who creates a safe, strong environment with well-defined personal boundaries so the child may develop as a separate individual.

From an essay by Don Dalton in the book *Healing Hearts*:

> [A parent needs] emotional support through the divorce process, and it becomes very easy to use the children. Children can become great empathizers and are very good at consoling and loving a hurt and grieving parent. The problem is, you are taking something from them that does not belong to you. Their happiness is paramount; you have to get yours somewhere else.

Children can be the perfect buddies: They can be manipulated into going where you want to go when you want to go. If they disagree, a parent can always withhold affection, withhold privileges, send them to their room, threaten abandonment—all of the manipulative strategies that a spouse or adult friend would never tolerate, but that can have a deep impact on a child. Children can be made very pliable and forced to bend to your will with these techniques.

The threat of abandonment is particularly effective if one parent has abandoned the child or has been driven away by intense litigation on the part of the custodial parent. Who else does the child have to turn to? The remaining parent is everything; potential abandonment now becomes the threat of losing all. A child can literally become an emotional hostage. Perhaps this is part of the reason some parents want sole custody of their children.

I've heard it said that, beginning on the day their child is born, the parents' job is to prepare the child to separate and become an individual. Both parent and child will struggle with this separation process over the years, for different reasons.

Resistance is a crucial component of growth. Take, for instance, our muscles in a workout—they will not grow without the resistance of weight and gravity.

Children also need resistance to grow. Their rebellious phases are crucial to their development as individuals. In a sense, they need us to be stodgy and conservative so they have something to push against and make the statement to themselves and the world that they are different from their parents and can go it alone.

If a parent does not offer that resistance, but instead becomes the buddy by using teen slang, wearing teen fashions, or driving a teenager's car, the child is competing with (and often losing to) the adult (who has had many more years of practice being an adolescent). The child is then operating in an emotional vacuum and cannot develop normally.

An extreme example of this is the mom who, driven by the fear of aging and wanting to be a girlfriend to her daughter and her daughter's friends, wears sexy, too-youthful clothing and flirts with her daughter's boyfriend.

Many divorcing adults exhibit symptoms of adolescence. Suddenly free of the shackles of marriage (much as they were breaking free from the shackles of their family in their teen years), they begin to experiment with drugs, alcohol, parties, and sex; they acquire "toys" such as new cars and boats; they work out obsessively at the gym to make themselves more desirable to a potential partner.

187

In divorce, one of the most common violations of the parent/child boundary is when the parent uses the child as a substitute for the absent parent. This is when the young son becomes "Mommy's little man" or "Dad's best buddy," when the daughter becomes "Mom's girlfriend" or "Daddy's little lady." The parent/child "couple" go on "dates" together to the movies or restaurants or engage in other activities the parent would normally do with a spouse or an adult friend.

This in no way implies that parents and children shouldn't do things together. In fact, opposite-gender parent/child relationships are crucial in preparing children for their future experiences with boyfriends and girlfriends. But when the child fills the void left by the absent spouse, it crosses over into murky, emotionally intrusive territory.

This can be particularly troubling when young children sleep with one or both of the divorced parents. Unquestionably, spending a night or two in their parents' bed can be reassuring during frightening events in children's lives, such as thunderstorms or earthquakes. But in divorce, children are too often manipulated to fill the void left by the absent spouse and become the sleeping partner of the single parent.

The key is to look at the bottom line of the parent's emotional needs. If the parent and child sleep and cuddle together at night because the parent is lonely, the child's body is being used for the physical comfort of the adult—and when an adult uses a child's body for comfort, it is abuse.

This issue can be especially hard on children if their parents are not cooperating with each other and have different household rules about significant issues such as sleep routines.

The rule is this: Same room, different bed is okay. Same room, same bed is not okay. If a child is traumatized by the divorce and is not able to sleep in his/her own bedroom, it is considered appropriate for the child to sleep in a parent's bedroom on a cot or sleeping bag for a period of time.

THE OTHER HOME

When your young child is at school, you have a reasonable expectation that he or she:

➤ will receive a balance of education plus physical exercise during the day,

➤ will be monitored for safety with a responsible adult always in close proximity,

➤ will receive medication on schedule per doctor's instructions,

➤ will be the subject of communication and cooperation between you and the child's caretakers,

➤ will not watch television for several hours a day,

➤ will not be fed large amounts of junk food,

➤ will not be bribed for affection with purchases of candy and toys or total relaxation of behavioral rules,

➤ will not be spanked or hit by an adult, or called stupid by an adult, or experience other such treatment,

➤ will not experience abuses such as sleeping with or cuddling with a teacher,

➤ will not be exposed to secondhand cigarette smoke for hours at a time (I've heard of a case where custody was withdrawn from a parent who refused to stop smoking around an asthmatic child),

➤ will not be allowed to watch films with sexual or violent content,

➤ will not have a teacher make disparaging remarks about you.

However, if these same issues are handled poorly around your child when he is in the other parent's home, you will not be able to do much about it. The little that you can do may result in a worse scenario for your child, notably the stress that comes from escalation of hostility and possible litigation between the parents.

This is the stuff that makes divorced parents crazy. But sometimes all one can do is take comfort in knowing that, at least for the time they are at school or under your care, your children are in a relatively positive environment.

Also remember that, if you were still married to the other parent, it is likely your children would be exposed to your ex-spouse's negative parenting traits 365 days a year.

Virtually all children try to manipulate differences between parents to their advantage with such things as "But Mom gives me two Popsicles!" or "Dad lets me watch television all day!"

When this happens in intact families, the two parents can often discuss it, chuckle about it, and learn to work together to minimize the age-old tactic of "divide and conquer."

But in divorce, if the two homes have different parenting styles and there is inadequate communication and cooperation between the parents, children's manipulative power can create huge problems. This is particularly true if that manipulation results in a contest between the parents as to who will buy more treats, allow more television hours, allow a later bedtime.

One day, when my daughter was six years old, she looked at me with big doe eyes and said, "Dad, I like your house and I like Mom's house. But I like Mom's house better because she has a dog. I'd like your house just as much if you got a dog, too." (I've often noted that the negotiating skills of the toughest attorney pale in comparison to those of a five- or six-year-old child.)

Sometimes it's tempting to give in to these bits of manipulation, but the answer has to be something like: "I'm glad you like Mom's house and glad that you like your dog. I understand that you wish there were a furry pet at Dad's house, too, but as you know, I'm allergic to animals and I can't have a pet in my house. You and I do a lot of other fun things together at my house, and we'll just have to concentrate on those."

Whether divorced or married, most parents who hold their ground and resist a child's manipulation will sooner or later find the child stomping off and shrieking, "I hate you!" or "You're mean!" or "I'm running away from home!"

When parents are working as a team, they can laugh this off. But for a parent in a high-conflict, noncommunicative divorce, these hurtful words can hit a raw nerve (which, of course, children know instinctively). The child can be especially cutting when he lashes out with something like, "I wish I lived at Mom's [or Dad's] house all the time!" Some divorced parents may feel the child's angry words echo the sentiments of the ex-spouse. They may even suspect that the other parent has been coaching the child.

Refusing to get sucked into the most-loved-parent contest may be difficult because of the little voice inside many divorced parents that says, "Choose me! Choose me!"

Divorced parents can be very sensitive about things their child says (or doesn't say) about the other home. It is another area where excessive demonizing of the ex-spouse can make a situation worse than it is.

You may interpret something positive the child says about the other parent as a betrayal, or you may worry that she likes the other parent more, or be concerned that the other parent's perception of you as a lousy person is validated in your child's eyes.

Conversely, being told something bad about the other parent may validate your demonizing of your ex. The ex-spouse's minor parenting flaws can be misinterpreted and distorted as abusive, then discussed with friends à la: "Little Johnny told me that [the other parent] did such and such. Can you believe [the other parent] did that?"

You cannot take at face value everything your child says about the other household.* Many stories will be untrue or exaggerated and, if not clarified, may lead to trouble. Parents' imaginations can run wild; ugly, untrue things may begin to appear in attorney letters or court documents, and the parental conflict escalates. You must communicate with the other parent directly—or in joint sessions with a counselor if need be—to clear these things up.

Unfortunately, some of the things a child says about the other home will be true. (Yes, the television may be on twenty-four hours a day.) At this point, you may need advice from a counselor about learning to accept that you will not be able to change a less-than-stellar situation in the other home.

If you truly believe that your child is experiencing neglect or abuse in the other home, you are morally compelled to take action through attorneys, courts, child protective services. Just be prepared for a be-

* At a beginning-of-the-school-year orientation, an elementary school teacher said the following to a group of parents: "If you promise to believe only half of everything you hear happens at school, I'll promise to believe only half of everything I hear happens at home."

wildering, painful, and expensive journey. It can also be a risky journey: There is always the chance that the court will order the child to spend *more* custody time in the other home.

Do not quiz your child about his life at the other home. Just make sure the line of communication between you and your child is open should he want to talk about anything at any time. Remember that conflicts she has with the other parent must, in most cases, be worked out between the two of them.

Do not in any way use a child as a conduit for communication with the other parent. Even when you discuss mundane issues with the other parent, it gives the child a sense of security to know he is being cared for by the most important team in his life.

Do not encourage the child to keep secrets about you or your home from the other parent. Only tell children what you want the other parent to know. Whatever you tell your child about sensitive issues in your life, you must tell the other parent—and the child must know that the conversation took place.

When you communicate openly with the other parent, you give children "permission" to speak freely to that parent about all aspects of their life, including the time they spend at your house. If you do not communicate openly with the other parent, the children often become guarded about expressing themselves for fear they may inadvertently tell something one parent was keeping a secret from the other. The children become emotional hostages.

It is the difference between:

(1) one parent who calls the other and says, "I've been dating someone for a few months now, and the relationship

is at the stage where I'm going to introduce him/her to [our child]. He/she is an accountant and has two children from a previous marriage" or

(2) a parent who has been dating someone for weeks, has been including him or her in social events with the child but has never mentioned any of it to the other parent—and then brings the new romantic interest to the child's birthday party unannounced. Such surprises are not constructive to the co-parenting relationship or to the child, who may be spending the birthday party with the emotional burden of wondering if the surprise will result in the parents having a fight during the party.

194

It is best that you communicate with the other parent about the children in most of the same ways you did when married. At the very least, you must discuss medical issues, school issues, after-school activities, vacations, dance and music lessons and recitals, and so forth. You should share basics about your personal life that might be sensitive issues for the children: general information about your dating, or major health issues that the children have been told about.

An even higher level of communication is important to help smooth children's transitions between homes, to give them routine and stability. Discuss their food preferences ("I discovered last week that Junior loves to eat raw broccoli!"), sleep routine, babysitters, changes in shoe and clothing sizes, rules about television and music listening, homework routine, and so forth. But this level of communication is not likely to happen if the parents are in a high-conflict divorce and are not communicating or cooperating with each other. Failure to communicate about these issues is known as "parallel parenting": The parents are moving along on parallel tracks that never intersect.

While the other parent is the primary person with whom you should frequently communicate about your child, he or she may be the last person who will talk to you. This is one of the tragic consequences of the selfishness common in high-conflict divorce. If you are unable to communicate directly with the other parent, do it through a mediator or counselor.

WHY DIDN'T YOU FIGHT FOR ME?

The child custody conflict between my ex-wife and me was so intense during the first several months of our divorce that I briefly considered surrendering my rights to joint custody for the sole purpose of removing my daughter from the conflict.

I thought of the biblical story in which, rather than have her baby cut in half by King Solomon, a mother offered to surrender the child to another woman who falsely claimed to be its mother.

This was one of the most gut-wrenching times of my life. It pained me to see my young daughter positioned in the middle of an ugly and unwarranted struggle—and it was obviously painful for her. Yet I feared that surrendering my joint-custody rights might not really solve the problem in the short or long term and that, once surrendered, parental rights might be difficult to regain. (Never forget that, in many states, custodial parents have the right to move their children out of state if they wish.)

I discussed the possibility of surrendering my wish for a shared-parenting child custody arrangement with a few friends who had been through the divorce process. They strongly and unanimously discouraged such a plan.

One friend in particular gave me the focus and determination I needed by relating his divorce experience. At the onset of his divorce, his ex-wife began to make rumblings about becoming the primary parent, with him having a limited parental role. He took a strong stand on the issue by stating, "Joint custody is the *only* issue in our divorce that is non-negotiable." This became my mantra.

However, the most compelling stories I heard, and the ones that gave me renewed determination, were from two other divorced friends. Both people (who don't know each other) had surrendered joint custody of their young daughters about twenty years ago for exactly the reason I was contemplating: to remove their daughters from being the center of conflict. When their daughters became young adults, both girls angrily confronted them with, "Why didn't you fight for me? Why didn't you want to be more involved in my life?"

As one of the parents sadly said to me, "You never want your child to ask you that question."

In cases such as this, the anger of the adult child of divorce may also be directed at the parent who "won" an unwarranted custody battle and had an active hand in disrupting one of the most important relationships a child can have.

197

If you remove the other parent from your child's life, you may have to answer to the child for that action someday in the future. Your child will probably figure out the truth about both parents, so the reasons for your actions will have to be very good ones and not just based on rage or desire for control.

Conversely, if you decide not to make every effort to be a part of your child's life, you may also have to answer to your child for that.

Children who are raised by only one parent often experience a sense of tremendous loss with the absence of the other parent. Friends of mine who experienced this as children of divorce describe it as very painful;

it creates a void in their heart that, on some level, is there forever. They often spend many years seeking ways to fill that emptiness. Even when absent parents reconnect with their children after years or decades of separation, they are not able to fully repair the damage their absence caused to the young child.

For a child, the death of a parent is painful but can be explained as an act of nature. However, when the parent is still alive but *chooses* not to be involved or is driven away by the other parent, the feeling of desertion can create a deep emotional wound.

Children need to feel valued and connected. Nothing can do this more than having an adult honor their life by spending time with them, listening to them, getting to know them.

If you are considering giving up custody to the other parent, remember that your child needs you. It may take great effort and sacrifice to remain involved in your child's life, but being a fully involved parent may be one of the most important contributions you can make to the world.

WARTS AND ALL

It's important that children get a realistic view of both parents. Children need to see how each parent handles stress, defeats, victories, joy, sadness, grumpiness. By getting a close, day-to-day view of the strengths and weaknesses of their parents, children can learn to make better life choices for themselves—especially with friends and romantic relationships. Divorce can offer clarity to children who spend extended one-on-one time with each parent.

It's tempting for us to parade our strengths in front of our children with the expectation that they will "respect" us, be proud of us, be amazed by us. But I believe that one of the most important—and challenging—gifts I can give my daughter is to let her experience my human weaknesses, too. By acknowledging, articulating, and—when appropriate—apologizing for my weaknesses, I hope I will give her a more realistic view of men. I hope this will increase her chances of making good choices in her relationships with them.

Children only get to know both parents "warts and all" by spending routine, day-to-day time with them over many years. This requires more than visits every other weekend. It requires shared parenting, with the child's time in each home being as close to 50/50 as possible.

Another unexpected wrinkle in "winning" sole or primary custody of a child is that the child may idealize the absent, or infrequently seen, parent. Not only can this be maddening for the custodial parent, but it is another way in which reality can become distorted for a child of divorce.

STEPPARENTS

The reality that an ex-spouse is seriously dating or marrying someone new may ignite many negative feelings in you (or your ex, if you're the one remarrying). The fact that someone finds your ex to be attractive or nice or loving may be difficult to stomach. It may also invalidate your demonization of your ex. ("Can't everyone in the world see what a louse he/she is?") Or it may signal the end of any chance of the reconciliation you may, perhaps unconsciously, have hoped for. Or it may mean having less impact on your ex-spouse; the emotional ties will diminish.

However, the big emotional button that remarriage may push is your fear of someone else caring for your children. This may drive you crazy, especially if you don't like or respect this other person. You may wonder if your child will be neglected, yelled at, punished too severely, or sexually, physically, or emotionally abused. Not only will the child's life be touched by the new stepparent, but the circle of people around your child becomes larger and more complicated with stepsiblings, stepgrandparents, stepcousins, and so on. For some parents, this can feel overwhelming if the child is very young and vulnerable.

Conversely, you may not want the new stepparent to be *too* good, for that can create fear that the child will prefer living at the other home—where there's lots of attention, there are really neat stepsiblings, the stepmom is a better cook or the stepdad is more interesting and exciting than you are.

You may fear that, if your child is old enough to choose a primary residence, he or she may choose the other home. You may fear that, if you are a single parent in litigation over child custody, the court will find that the child's needs are better met in a "stable" two-parent home. (Don't lose sleep over this fear—it's not usually a major factor in child custody disputes.) You may also fear that a career change for your ex's new spouse may mean that both the couple and the children will move to a different city, state, or country.

Sometimes parents who remarry use these fears to cruelly jab the emotions of their ex-spouse. This is another form of using children as a weapon.

Stepparents can sometimes be beneficial. As one child of divorce said, "I'm so lucky! I've got four parents who love me and care for me."

In some cases, a stepparent may act as a buffer between the hostile parents—a safe go-between for exchanging the children or discussing school or routine scheduling plans around after-school activities. This can result in a very constructive team effort.

But this can be tricky and perhaps should only be a temporary plan. The long-term goal should be direct communication between the two parents.

If, however, a stepparent is a hindrance to the custody routine and becomes involved in the conflict, the biological parent married to him or her must remove that stepparent from the custody and transition picture and communicate directly with the other parent.

There is also the issue of how children address their new stepparent. Using "Mom" or "Dad" is usually not a good idea; the biological mom or dad will probably take a dim view of this.* Addressing the

---

* Note the clause that specifically addresses this issue in the sample separation agreement at the end of this book.

stepparent by first name or nickname may be the best option. In any case, the issue should be negotiated so that all—especially the child and biological parents—are comfortable with the arrangement.

It's also important to consider the point of view of a stepparent, for marrying someone who is in a high-conflict shared-parenting arrangement is not a cakewalk. It means marrying into a relationship with a hostile ex-spouse, caring for some other person's children (perhaps being compared with the biological parent who is the ex-spouse), perhaps being affected by spousal or child-support payments paid to the ex-spouse.* These issues and others like them can create a major strain on a new marriage.

Stepparent issues are complex and go beyond the scope of this book. You can find other books that deal with this in more detail by contacting the Stepfamily Association of America at 1-800-735-0329 or the Stepfamily Foundation at 1-800-SKY-STEP. Or consult with a therapist who specializes in divorce issues.

However, I will leave you with this: When a friend of mine remarried recently (he is the father of two children from his first marriage), he and his new wife wrote vows that they read to each other during the wedding ceremony. As part of her vows, his new wife said the following before all in attendance: "I promise to love and care for your children and promise to always honor their mother."

Rarely have I witnessed words making such a strong impact on a gathering of people. The air was electric as a wave of good feeling surged through the room. These were life-affirming words, words of grace. They set the standard for us all.

---

* Be sure to get legal advice about protecting a new spouse's income from being included in calculations for spousal or child-support payments.

A QUICK LIST OF DOS AND DON'TS

If both parents follow these guidelines, the divorce will be smoother for all concerned. Most of it falls under the Golden Rule we learned as children: "Treat others as you want to be treated."

➤ Stay focused on constructive actions. Avoid litigation unless it is absolutely necessary. Remember that the level of conflict in your divorce will have a direct impact on your children—the higher the divorce conflict, the more damaging it is to them.

➤ Make sure your children know that they are not the cause of the divorce.

➤ Reassure your children that they will be cared for, that both parents will be okay after the divorce, that they will see both parents.

➤ Keep your promises to your children and to the other parent. Show up on time for home transitions, school functions, recitals, and so forth.

➤ Honor your obligations regarding spousal and child support payments. If you are the payer, pay on time. If you are the receiver, use child-support money for the children's welfare.

➤ Don't use your children as a conduit for communication between parents. Even if seemingly mundane subjects need to be discussed, children are reassured and comforted to know that their parents are communicating directly in a civil, businesslike manner.

➤ Don't use your children as a weapon against your ex-spouse in any way.

➤ Don't use your children as spies to tell you about goings-on at the other home.

➤ Do not try to buy the love of your children.

➤ If there is a high degree of hostility between you and your ex, consider having the custody transitions take place at a neutral, public place that is fun for the children, such as a playground, a family restaurant, or one of the many church- , YMCA- or YWCA-sponsored transition centers around the nation created for just this purpose.

➤ Tell your children the truth, but keep it simple. For instance, if the other parent has a drug or alcohol addiction, speak of it in a compassionate, nonjudgmental manner. Don't make any negative comments about the other parent.

➤ Redefine your relationship with your ex-spouse, keeping in mind that you will always be the parents of your children.

➤ Do not brainwash your children by subtly erasing references to the other parent (no photos of the other parent, no conversation about the other parent, not allowing the children phone access to the other parent) or by overtly making derogatory comments about the other parent. Instruct your friends and family to abide by this as well.

➤ Don't put the children in the position of having to choose one parent over the other.

➤ Don't discuss divorce-related financial or legal issues in front of the children.

➤ Honor the other parent's time with and without the children. Don't schedule activities that will impact the other parent's custody time without his or her consent. Pick up and drop off the child on time so the other parent may honor commitments he/she has when the child is with you.

➤ You can be friendly with your children, but you cannot be friends. You are the parent. Show love to your children by giving them predictability and stability with well-defined rules, limits, and personal boundaries.

➤ Don't let your children take care of your emotional needs. Use adult friends or a therapist to find your own comfort.

➤ *Do* find comfort and support for yourself, for it will make you a healthier, more available parent.

➤ Have realistic expectations about your divorce journey. You will probably feel many conflicting emotions about your ex-spouse. You will have ups and downs. Accept that it usually takes a few years to heal.

➤ If you enter a rebound romantic relationship after separation, proceed slowly. You are emotionally vulnerable, and it may be a while before you are in a good frame of mind for making important life decisions.

CHILDREN'S RIGHTS COUNCIL

CRC is a group of men and women working together to promote education, support of parents, and legislation that will make divorce and custody easier on children. The organization's definition of families is broad, yet it works hard to address issues of specific groups. For instance, a CRC website is dedicated solely to giving information and support to never-married parents. I urge you to join CRC. It has only one agenda: putting the needs of children first when parents separate.

Reprinted from the Children's Rights Council newsletter, *Speak Out for Children,* spring 1999:

> The Children's Rights Council (CRC) is a nationwide, non-profit IRS 501(c)(3) children's rights organization based in Washington, D.C.
>
> CRC works to strengthen families through education and advocacy. We favor family formation and family preservation, but if families break up, or are never formed, we work to assure a child the frequent and continuing contact with two parents and an extended family the child would normally have during a marriage. Our motto is "The Best Parent Is Both Parents."
>
> For the child's benefit, CRC favors parenting education before marriage, during marriage, and for parents who are unwed or separated. We work to demilitarize divorce between parents who are involved in marital disputes, substituting con-

ciliation and mediation for the adversarial process, and providing for emotional and financial child support. We work to strengthen fragile families of children whose parents are unwed. We also favor school-based programs for children at risk.

Formed in 1985 by concerned parents who have more than 40 years collective experience in custody reform and early childhood education, CRC has chapters in 32 states and two national affiliate organizations: Mothers Without Custody (MW/OC) and the Stepfamily Association of America (SAA).

Prominent professionals in the fields of religion, law, social work, psychology, child care, education, business, and government comprise our Advisory Panel.

For further information about CRC membership, publications, cassettes, catalog, and services, write: CRC, 300 "I" Street N.E., Suite 401, Washington, D.C. 20002-4389; phone (202) 547-6227; fax (202) 546-4CRC (4272).

207

The CRC home page is *http://www.gocrc.com*
Speak Out for Children is published four times a year.

THE AFTERMATH AND OTHER CONSIDERATIONS

Scarcely anything which I was taught to believe lasted.
And everything I was taught to believe impossible had
happened. [Victory had indeed been] bought so dear as to
be indistinguishable from defeat."

— Winston Churchill reflecting on World War I,
from *The Last Lion*, by William Manchester

HEALING

Healing is achieved in many different ways. It can begin at the outset of a divorce and be a part of all phases of the divorce if you allow it to be. However, the lion's share of healing is usually accomplished after the divorce is finalized.

Healing involves acknowledging a loss, grieving that loss, learning from it, then discovering ways to move forward positively in life. In particular, it means learning what things you can control and letting go of the things you cannot. For more on this, I recommend Judith Viorst's books *Necessary Losses* and *Imperfect Control*.

Healing can begin at the start of a conflict if there is a concerted attempt to make constructive, life-affirming choices during the conflict. You'll probably make some errors in divorce, but try not to let them be actions done in bad faith or out of spite. The most healing gift you can give yourself and your children is being able to walk away from your divorce with a clean heart knowing that you did not engage in dirty tricks, did not try to hurt or punish your child's other parent, did not betray marital intimacies to gain strategic advantage, did not use your children as negotiating currency or weapons, did not try to undermine the child's relationship with the other parent.

Healing means keeping your integrity and moral center during even the most immoral conflict. You cannot control another person's actions, but you can control how you react to them. You have the moral power to choose not to retaliate in kind against dirty tricks. Rise above it all with grace.

Healing means acknowledging and accepting your mistakes, and apologizing for them when appropriate. Your apology may not be accepted, but you cannot control how another person will respond to your gesture. You can only do what is right and send that goodness out into the world.

Each person has an individual time frame for healing; your true friends will allow you the time you need. Avoid people who are critical or judgmental about your healing process.

True healing is not easy and does not mean always feeling good. Sometimes healing requires painful self-examination of your motives and actions. The object of self-examination is to identify patterns of unhealthy choices we make in life and then avoid those same unhealthy choices in the future—such as when entering a new romantic relationship.

214

I do not believe that healing is necessarily avoiding conflict or anger. Anger can be constructive when channeled positively into determination.

For instance, if I had not done everything in my power to ensure that I remained an integral part of my young daughter's daily life, I would feel as though I had broken my moral bond with her.

Giving up custody might have left me wealthier, but it would not have been the right choice—the healing choice—for my daughter and me.

For me, healing was trying to understand what had happened to my life, to make sense of the tragedy and conflict, and find ways to turn destruction into something constructive (this book, for example).

It was about getting through the conflict with as much grace as possible. Most of the time I believe I succeeded, but not always.

I am fortunate to have friends and family who helped me heal. They listened to me vent and analyze the events of my life, let me cry, gave me a safe, sympathetic, nonjudgmental place in which to express my feelings of anger, sadness, bewilderment, grief, and concern for my daughter's welfare.

I healed by participating in therapy. Here I was also fortunate to work with two therapists who maintained a good balance: They were sympathetic, but they also challenged me.

I healed by swimming, walking on the beach, enjoying good food, wine, gentle music, and conversation with friends; by being open to a new life as a single person and finding ways to adjust positively to the days when I wasn't with my daughter; by becoming involved (slowly and carefully) with a kindhearted, patient woman who helped restore my faith and trust.

LOOK ON THE BRIGHT SIDE

When we experience loss, we must acknowledge and mourn it; denying it isn't healthy. Eventually we work through the pain: The loss is not in our thoughts every minute of every day, and we once again begin to experience happiness and hope. Sometimes this takes months or years.

If I assess my life experience as it stands right now (at age forty-six), it is nothing like the hopes and dreams I pictured for my future when I was a child. When I felt discouraged after my divorce began, it helped me to look at my "reality lists" from time to time, to see my life in broader perspective.

A list of my losses or negatives of the past few years:

➤ My infant son passed away.

➤ By age thirty-eight I'd lost both parents and all four grandparents.

➤ My marriage ended.

➤ I do not see my young daughter three or four days a week.

➤ My daughter was caught in the middle of a high-conflict divorce.

➤ As a result of my journey through the family law system, I've lost part of my sense of justice, truth, and faith in human nature.

➤ It will take years for me to recover financially from my divorce: I've lost the equity in my home, I've refinanced the home and car, and have taken out lines of credit to buy time to recover financially and support two households instead of one, savings that should have been my daughter's college fund have been depleted.

➤ I lost three years of my life in litigation and conflict. I would have preferred those years to be spent in creative, peaceful pursuits; my time on earth is finite.

➤ According to statistical averages, the divorce has reduced my life expectancy by at least two years.

➤ The degree of conflict and stress in my life for the past several years puts me in the "high risk" group for disability, health, and life insurance.

➤ I lost a lifelong dream—perhaps an overly romanticized, unrealistic dream—of a happy marriage to one person for decades, creating a family history together, caring for each other, watching our children and grandchildren grow up.

In short, I've experienced a fair amount of pain, loss, grief, and stress. To cope with this, I acknowledge the sorrow, shame, anger, frustration, and confusion that accompany unpleasant life events such as these. Then I concentrate on rebuilding my life by acknowledging the good, hopeful parts of my existence. I'm certainly not cheerful all the time, but as I journey through life, I'm able to find gifts that probably would have eluded me if I'd stayed married. These are such things as:

➤ I have a much closer relationship with my daughter. When my marriage ended, it was difficult for me to

believe the many divorced dads who told me this
would be true, but it is.

➤ I am offered the adventure of building new hopes and
dreams with a new life partner.

➤ On the days my daughter is at her mom's house, I
have free time as a single person to enjoy adult dinner
parties with stimulating conversation, go to orchestra
concerts, read books, exercise, swim, listen to music,
get a massage. Doing these things makes me more
available in energy and spirit for my daughter; my life
with her is enriched.

➤ My home is a place of emotional safety, comfort, and
peace; tension is gone.

➤ Activities with my daughter, the food I cook, the
friends I invite over no longer need to be negotiated
with a partner. There are fewer complications; life can
be more spontaneous.

➤ There is hope in my life, something that wasn't there
for me in my marriage.

Social scientists tell us that the healthiest and most satisfying existence is being in a happy, fulfilling marriage. Since I'm not in that category of "happily married" people, I am content to view myself as living the "second best" existence for the time being. I feel sorriest for
those who stay in miserable marriages—doing so can kill the soul.

As I noted before, we cannot always control events in our life, but we
can usually control how we react to those events. We can be paralyzed
with negative emotions (and it's normal if you experience negative

emotions during divorce), or we can eventually move forward with determination, creativity, and grace.

It's like accidentally dropping a carton of eggs. While sunny-side up may no longer be possible, you now have the opportunity to create a mighty fine omelet.

You will get through your divorce. It will be difficult and painful, but there will probably be a point where you'll wonder how you stayed in the marriage for as long as you did. The list of good things in your life will get longer as each year passes.

ORDER OUT OF CHAOS

As your marriage dissolves, it may feel as though your entire world is crumbling around you. All the years and energy you invested in the partnership may now seem to have been wasted.

The hopes and promises of "happily ever after" with which you've been programmed since childhood have not come true.

The person who was your best, most-trusted friend—the person you swore to love, honor, and cherish for the rest of your life—may now be your worst enemy.

What was supposed to be your life's "safe zone"—your family and home—may now be shattered.

Your life is in chaos.

Humans do not like chaos. When it envelops us, most of us struggle to find out a) why it happened and b) how to avoid it in the future.

Many people who go through divorce spend months or years bouncing between the emotions of sadness, anger, and bewilderment asking, "What in the world happened!? I worked so hard to create a good marriage!"

We try to superimpose order on chaos by pointing to specific events to explain what might have happened—or by blaming our ex-spouse. We seek answers through religion, therapy, self-help books, talking with friends.

The people around you may also try to impose order on the chaos in your life, to concoct explanations or reasons why you have experienced divorce. ("Your marriage fell apart because . . . .) Sometimes this is helpful; usually it is not (especially if they include the phrase ". . . fell apart because you . . ."). You may need to distance yourself from those who say such things.

I've heard it said that my parents' generation, those who grew up during the Depression and World War II, experienced lives of tremendous chaos and uncertainty. They reacted to that in the 1950s and 1960s by trying to create perfect suburban families and homes, by working hard to shield their children—us—from the reality of chaos. While well-intentioned, this strategy didn't necessarily prepare us for accepting and coping with the chaos and tragedies of life. Instead, it gave us the illusion of control, the illusion that, if we worked hard enough, we could accomplish anything.

221

For instance, I have a friend who never attended a funeral until he was in his late thirities and was deeply shocked by the experience. This is not uncommon in my generation. Contrast this with society as recently as a few decades ago, when witnessing—and having to cope with—sickness, disaster, and death was a normal part of a young person's life.

My generation was also raised in a time when science and medicine came of age. They began to protect us from the chaos: Polio was eradicated, human hearts were transplanted, causes of cancer were identified. We embraced these successes and projected them onto other areas of our lives, manufacturing false hope that all of life could be arrayed in neat cause-and-effect lists.

Sometimes we simply have to accept that there is no "because"; that much of life is chaos and there's little or nothing we can do about it. This can be difficult to accept. Sometimes the only thing we can do with chaos is to deal with it as gracefully as possible.

For more on this, I recommend reading *When Bad Things Happen to Good People* by Harold S. Kushner.

ON THE REBOUND

Divorce is rejection. It can be a crushing blow to your self-esteem and your perception of yourself as a kind, thoughtful, loving, sexually desirable person. What better way to take the sting out of the rejection than by rebounding into the arms of a new lover who can validate that perception?

The freedom that often comes after a couple has separated can be very heady. You may dive into your new single life with gusto, acquiring a new boat, new car, new furniture, new friends, new clothes, new hairstyle. In many ways it seems like a second adolescence, not only because of the liberation from family members who may have wanted you to conform to their lifestyle (your parents when you were younger, your spouse when you were married), but also because of a certain amount of flailing about that many divorced people do as they struggle to redefine themselves. In the midst of this newfound freedom, you may suddenly find yourself in a romantic relationship. While this may have some pluses, it might also be thought of as jumping out of the frying pan into the fire.

Sometimes a rebound relationship is a result of fear—fear of being alone, fear of not being validated as an attractive person, fear of not being able to support oneself financially.

Slow down. Take time to recover from your marital split and to rediscover yourself as a single person before entering into a new love relationship. Moving too quickly into a new relationship can make you emotionally vulnerable. Keep in mind that you may not be in a good state of mind to be making important choices in life, that a rebound relationship has very little chance of long-term success.

If you cannot refrain from a rebound relationship, at the very least shield your children from it. While you may be ready for new love, they probably are not ready to see you being affectionate with—certainly not sleeping with—a new person anytime soon. Your new romance can make them vulnerable, too, especially if they become emotionally attached to your new friend (who may not be around in a few weeks).

Before you inform your children about the new relationship, it is best that you tell your ex-spouse about it. All you need to say is, "I've been dating someone for a few months and believe it's time for me to introduce him/her to the children. His/her name is _____." It's best to relay a few basics about the person, such as his or her profession and whether or not he/she also has children who your children will be meeting soon.

Your ex-spouse may react negatively to this news, but some of that is to be expected; it can be a blow to your ex's pride, or he/she may be concerned about how the children will be treated by this new adult in their lives. You cannot control your ex-spouse's reaction. You can only control your own action—which is to do the right thing and communicate with your children's other parent.

Make sure your children know that you have had this conversation so they don't fear betraying you by talking about your new love with the other parent. Remember: You must never do anything (or omit anything) that will make your children cautious about expressing themselves around their other parent.

Again, here is the rule regarding important issues in your household: Whatever you tell the children, you must tell the other parent.

Try to take time after separation to learn about yourself, to learn the reasons (good and bad) you chose your previous spouse, to become emotionally centered as a single person. Then begin a new love relationship from a position of inner strength and wisdom. Not only will this approach probably serve you best, but your children may learn from your example so that they make better relationship choices in the future.

Check with your attorney about dating before your divorce is formalized. He or she will probably recommend that you be discreet about it. While it's unlikely that a court will punish you for dating now that your marriage is over, flaunting your new love in your ex's face or around the children will likely escalate the conflict and create unnecessary obstacles to finalizing the divorce quickly and inexpensively.

A MORE REALISTIC VIEW OF MARRIAGE

How many truly happily married couples have you known in your life?

I've posed this question to dozens of people, and most can only recall knowing three or four couples they would consider "happily married."

Happy marriages are two people who respect each other, are affectionate with each other, genuinely seem to enjoy each other's company and conversation. After years of marriage, they can still make each other laugh out loud with a witty comment. These are the couples who, after having been apart for only a few hours during the day, greet each other before dinner with a smile and a hug and chatter on like old friends who haven't spoken in months. These are the couples who remain committed to each other through the tough times—and gain respect for each other for having done so.

When we talk about the fact that approximately fifty percent of marriages end in divorce, many people may assume that the other fifty percent of marriages are happy. To the contrary, I would guess that many of the people in these fifty percent of intact marriages muddle through life year after year without deep love and joy. Perhaps they tolerate their spouse's infidelity because they want to keep up appearances, or they feel that remaining in the marriage gives them financial security, or they want continued daily oversight of the children at any cost, or they are terrified of being single again, or they are content with the philosophy of "better the devil you know." Whatever the reason, they have renegotiated the marital contract.

We all probably have a different and ever-changing definition of happiness. Perhaps over the years we begin to settle for contentment, or safety, or at least familiarity. Doing this is renegotiating the personal "hopes and dreams" contract with ourselves. But there is sometimes a limit to these renegotiations of the marital contract, and when that limit is reached, the marriage ends.

A minister friend of mine once said that he wasn't sure marriage was ever designed to last forty or fifty years. Marriage was a lifetime vow, but the institution evolved at a time when lifetimes were short. Centuries ago, couples typically married and conceived children in their mid-teens, then died ten, fifteen, or twenty years later. Today's long lifespans, plus the overwhelming number of life choices we have—changing careers, changing religions, changing living locations, changing hobbies, changing philosophies, changing social and economic status—all place pressures on partnerships that never existed before. Added to this is the fact that these changes can happen very quickly in today's world.

In mankind's past (and in some present-day cultures), marriage was often strictly a business arrangement. It boiled down to two young people who, having been brought together as a result of agreements made by their parents, worked together in a partnership just to survive and pass on genetic material to their offspring. Eventually, as basic survival became easier, we were afforded the luxury of considering the elements of romance and personal choice as part of the marital agreement. By the time my generation came along, we were fed a

227

steady diet of stories and movies that dangled the unrealistic promise of living happily ever after. When a marriage crumbles, the fall from these lofty, idealistic heights, with the subsequent feelings of failure and shame, can be devastating.

Perhaps we would be better served by using some middle ground as a point of reference for life's hopes and dreams—by acknowledging that a good marriage contains intoxicating romance and friendship, but that it is also a business partnership.

I often wonder what I'm going to tell my young daughter about marriage when she reaches her teens and early twenties. I don't want to burst her bubble of romantic ideals, but I also don't want to be dishonest with her by failing to discuss the realities of life. With the longer lifespans of her generation, there is a high probability that she, through divorce or widowhood, will have two or three marital partners. I view discussing this as I view educating her about the realities of riding in a car. While I pray she never experiences a car accident, there is a fairly high probability that she will. I can only hope my efforts in educating her about safe driving and wearing a seat belt will lessen the consequences for her.

Marriage requires great courage and hope—and perhaps a necessary bit of delusional thinking as well. After all, how many other things would humans agree to participate in that had a fifty percent chance of ending in disaster?

In all human endeavors there is a natural tension between the needs of the individual and the needs of the group. There are guidebooks, seminars, classes, and rituals that define and make more workable the structure of human groups such as sports teams, surgical teams, music ensembles, and corporations. But the most important partnerships we have—marriage and parenting—we leave mostly to chance (and hormones). The implied contracts that are part of these partnerships are usually not clearly articulated; we often delude ourselves about the realities and consequences of our human interactions.

For instance, perhaps unmarried people of child-bearing age should wear underwear that has a simple contract printed on the front. This contract, which must be signed before engaging in sex, might state:

> If an unplanned pregnancy should result from this sexual encounter, I agree to abide by the laws of this state regarding child-support payments. I am committed to a 50/50 shared parenting: I promise to consult the other parent in all matters regarding our child's upbringing. I promise not to move our child from the city where the other parent resides without the consent of that other parent.

229

Signed: _____

This contractual underwear is absurd; we laugh at the thought of two people actually signing such a contract. Yet it articulates a realistic situation: In most states, each time a couple—married or unmarried—has sexual relations, they are, in the eyes of the law, signing the above contract.

This is an example of a realistic life contract that we often choose to ignore. It is a sobering counterpoint to the romantic intoxication of an intimate sexual encounter. It is the sort of reality we need to impart to young adults. Perhaps by offering more life-skills courses—with an emphasis on clearly articulating the contracts of marriage, parenthood, coping with day-to-day real-life situations—we can create a happier, healthier life track for our society.

When I've spoken with couples who have been happily married for thirty, forty, or fifty years and have asked them the secrets to their success, the word "luck" is always at or near the top of the list.

I've observed that these good marriages often seem to be composed of two strong individuals who do not give themselves over to their partner to the degree that they feel resentful. They have an equal standing in the partnership and retain good personal boundaries around their individuality; each has a full life doing things that do not involve the other spouse.

As women achieve more financial equality, it means that both partners are together by choice; neither can be held financially hostage to the other. This is ultimately good for many reasons. It means that men may feel less pressure to "perform" financially, will have more time to spend with their children, and may live longer lifespans due to decreased stress. Perhaps it also means that divorce will be less of a financial battlefield.

Partnership contracts are already being redefined. For instance, more and more widowed or divorced people of retirement age find themselves in a new monogamous relationship, yet choose not to remarry. In many of these cases, both have financial resources, retirement plans, Social Security benefits, investments, car, and so on, and they remain single as a way to keep their assets completely separate. In some cases, even though partners are with each other almost daily, they keep their own houses rather than live together.

Any discussion of realistic, clearly defined relationship contracts leads to the subject of prenuptial agreements.

The popular economic advisor Suze Orman recommends prenuptial agreements for everyone. They shouldn't be viewed as a loss of romance, she says, but as an acknowledgment that a marriage may end someday. When two people are entering marriage, they are more likely to be reasonable, generous, and fair about possible future division of assets than when they are mired in the anger and craziness of divorce.

One family law professional* has even proposed that, from the beginning of the marriage, couples should make regular contributions to a savings account that is earmarked as a "divorce fund." If they never use it for that, they're richer in their retirement years. If they do dissolve the marriage along the way, it may help soften the financial impact.

A "prenup" is fairly standard when one or both parties enter the marriage with substantial financial assets. It is made to clearly define separate and community property and to spell out the manner in which these will be handled during the marriage and in the event of a divorce.

However, perhaps we should consider prenups for all marriages, with renegotiations every year or so to minimize those little issues that sometimes fester and become big issues. If nothing else, discussing marital contracts would help clarify the assumptions that so often cause difficulties in marriage; it might prevent conflict.

Perhaps the prenup would contain a parenting clause articulating the amount of involvement each parent will have in raising the children if the marriage stays intact, and define a basic plan or "mission statement" for cooperative shared parenting if the marriage ends.

For instance, in case of divorce, the prenup contract might include the promise to stay in close geographic proximity so the children will have frequent and regular contact with both parents and have the stability of their friends and community to help them deal with the di-

231

* Jed H. Abraham, *From Courtship to Courtroom*, Bloch Publishing, 2000.

vorce. It might also contain promises to seek counseling when the marriage is not going well and to participate in counseling and mediation if the marriage ends and co-parenting conflicts arise. In general, this means making the moral, selfless decision to put the needs of the children first.

Social institutions, such as marriage, are often resistant to change. But life is about constant and inevitable change—and no two people in a partnership will change and grow in the same way. Living a conscious, aware, examined life in which issues are discussed, clarified, and negotiated—sometimes through counseling—can help keep changes from creating irreparable rifts in a relationship.

GREAT EXPECTATIONS

We commonly make gestures to other people with the expectation of a response. We cook a special meal for a loved one expecting that the effort will be honored with a smile, a kind word, or a hug. We make an effort to do something we know will benefit our children and, naturally, we hope for some kind of acknowledgment that they appreciate it.

But giving is not true giving when it has strings attached; our giving gestures lose integrity when we expect something in return. Moreover, when we make a kind gesture or express our feelings in the hope of a response, we make ourselves emotionally vulnerable. However, when we do those things without expectations, we are not vulnerable.

Parenting is like that. I tell my young daughter dozens of times a day how wonderful she is. Sometimes I use words ("You are so wonderful," "I'm so proud of you for how kind you are to other people," "I'm such a lucky dad"), but mostly I tell her in unspoken ways—a smile, a gentle pat, a hug, showing interest in the stories or opinions she shares with me each day, holding her hand when we go for a walk after dinner. Most of the time she loves hearing it and responds positively; sometimes she seems about to burst with joy at hearing my words and throws her arms around my neck and holds me tight. On other occasions she couldn't care less, and my gestures dissolve into thin air. But that's okay. I love her no matter what—this is unconditional love (and one of the greatest life lessons my daughter has given to me).

Sometimes it is very difficult to give without receiving that reward—but then I remind myself that the expectation of a reward is about *my* needs and has nothing to do with my daughter's needs.

This same principle holds true for how you handle your divorce. You must find ways, even small ways, to honor the other parent. If you are not honored in return, it doesn't matter. You can only control your own actions.

Reasonable, generous, ethical proposals and gestures you make to your soon-to-be-ex-spouse may fall on deaf ears—or may be met with suspicion that you're only being nice because you want something. This can be frustrating if you're trying to get your family through the divorce with as little damage as possible and you're not getting any cooperation from your ex-partner—in fact, he/she may be passively or actively sabotaging your efforts in an effort to punish you, to stay tied to you in a negative way.

It's hard—sometimes very hard—to have your fair and reasonable efforts be misinterpreted or rebuffed. But you must still proceed through your divorce ethically. Continue to do what is right without the expectation of any kind of reward from your ex-spouse, your ex's attorney, or the judge's decision.

And, most important, without expectations of any reward from your children. At times in your divorce, well-meaning friends may offer comfort by saying something to the effect of, "In the future, your children will know the truth about your kindness and commitment to them." While it feels good when our children acknowledge our stellar parenting, it cannot be our motivation for acting with integrity in the divorce.

As we mature, one of the losses many of us experience is the loss of a sense of fairness (divorce can play a big role here). This sense of fairness usually doesn't have a foundation in reality; it is a product of childhood fantasies and expectations that are rooted in the storybook "happily-ever-after" endings we learn. It also comes from the simplistic religious teachings many of us are exposed to throughout childhood—the reward of heaven if we are good boys and girls.

But perhaps heaven is contentment and self-respect, the ability to look in the mirror and say, "I lived a good day today. I tried to do my small part in making the world a better place (or at least by not making it any worse)."

This should be reward enough—no expectation of receiving a pat on the back from anybody else (although it feels delicious when that happens). Think back to the quote from Rabbi Harold Kushner earlier in this book: "What I believe is that the most precious thing in the sight of God is the good deed freely chosen."

Freely chosen—without expectations.

A PUBLIC HEALTH AND A MENTAL HEALTH ISSUE

Divorce should often be regarded as a public health and a mental health issue rather than as a legal issue.

A lot of divorce litigation is driven by emotional abuses: vindictiveness, rage, manipulating children against the other parent, sabotaging joint custody. These are mental health issues, not legal issues. They are not effectively addressed by the family law system, which is steered largely by professionals whose training is in law, not mental health.

The loss to our society caused by prolonged, high-conflict divorce litigation is staggering. Parents and children lose years of productive life in work and school as a result of divorce-related depression, rage, and financial hardship.

A recent study of small businesses done by the Ohio Psychological Association found that divorce and other marital problems had a more negative impact on the workplace than drug or alcohol abuse.

Divorce is an emotionally volatile time in which the parties involved may not be capable of making responsible decisions about the long-term welfare of their lives and the lives of their children. Many litigants cannot see beyond the rage of the moment.

For this reason, I believe society needs to intervene in high-conflict divorces more frequently and more long-term. Here are the steps I believe are crucial:

1. De-escalate the situation with closer monitoring of client and attorney behavior. Scrutiny of behavior carries the threat of accountability. This accountability must be in the form of definite, quick, firm consequences for such offenses as committing perjury or denying a parent's access to children without cause.

2. Mandate a strong, rarely flexible legal presumption of joint custody to discourage unwarranted custody disputes and to rid the family law system of the concept of "winning" or "losing" children. At the very least, custody arrangements should mirror each parent's proportion of child care before separation, with the near-future goal of having the child spend at least forty percent of the time in each home.

   Research overwhelmingly shows us that children who have regular and frequent contact with both parents do much better than children raised by only one parent.

   Recent research also reveals that states that have legislated a presumption of joint custody after divorce also have the lowest divorce rates.

3. Separate financial issues and child custody issues so one cannot be used as negotiating leverage against the other.

4. Help guide high-conflict litigants through the first couple of difficult, volatile years with frequent, long-term, court-ordered mediation, co-parenting classes, and individual or joint counseling.

   As noted earlier, Virginia, Utah, Connecticut, and New Hampshire have passed legislation that requires divorcing parents to attend parent-education classes. The purpose of the classes is to sensitize the parents about how

237

their behavior during and after the divorce will impact their children. In Utah, this legislation has been so successful that eighty percent of those who attend believe a similar program *before* marriage would be helpful.

5. Offer creative incentives to motivate divorcing parents to avoid litigation. For instance, make a certain amount of divorce mediation and counseling fees tax-deductible.

6. Mandate that both litigants must pay a portion of divorce costs, so that a rageful client and an unethical attorney do not keep litigation alive by assuming that the primary wage-earner will pay fees for both sets of attorneys. Doing this will diminish unnecessary litigation.

7. Focus on children's rights. Unless legitimate issues of abuse or endangerment exist, give children frequent and regular contact with both parents (whether they are divorced or never married), and frequent and regular contact with grandparents and extended family. Shield children from exposure to high levels of conflict between parents. Keep children from being moved to another city, state, or country by one parent against the other's wishes.

8. Create more uniformity in the states' divorce laws. Marriage and divorce are historically state-regulated, but there is currently a confusing legal patchwork of fifty different sets of laws. Greater uniformity would make it easier to initiate national dialogue to find solutions to the societal problems caused by divorce.

Adopting these ideas would, I am convinced, reduce the costs of divorce to the state, to the litigants, and— most importantly—to the children.

PART VII

NUTS AND BOLTS OF DIVORCE

CHOOSING AN ATTORNEY

If you've read the previous chapters describing ethical attorneys vs. unethical attorneys, you have a pretty good idea of how to differentiate between styles of lawyering.

I have been told that clients tend to gravitate to attorneys with similar moral values. If you are a vindictive person out to do harm to your ex-spouse, you may seek an unethical or "killer" attorney. If you are a life-affirming person who wants to get on with your life, assertively protect your interests, but do as little damage as possible to your ex and your children, you will seek an ethical attorney.

Begin your search with personal recommendations from trusted friends who have professional knowledge of an ethical, experienced attorney who specializes in family law. If you can canvass friends who are themselves attorneys, so much the better.

If yours is a lower-income family, you may find legal-aid services in the yellow pages, or check legal-aid listings on your state bar association's website or at a public library. Some large legal firms do limited pro bono (free) work as a public service.

Interview a few attorneys; do some research about them through your state bar (most state bar associations have websites), checking for the number of disciplinary actions against them. Look up their rating in the *Martindale-Hubbell Law Directory* at a library or on the Internet.

Be wary of attorneys who advertise. In the legal community, advertising is considered somewhat tasteless and is usually done by firms that concentrate on volume business. Volume business doesn't often equate with individual attention; in other words, you may end up having your case handled by junior legal staff or by several different attorneys and may not get the personal attention to detail that you deserve.

A good client/attorney relationship is one of regular personal interaction and individual attention. As the attorney talks to you over weeks or months, he/she will get an accurate picture of you, your ex-spouse, your children, and other details of your life that may help your case. This familiarity and detailed knowledge of your situation will be beneficial during settlement negotiations—and may be crucial if your case goes to trial.

As you interview attorneys, don't be afraid to ask questions. You're on the right track when you meet an attorney who spends half an hour of free consultation time with you, listens to you, answers your questions patiently, is not interrupted by assistants during the meeting, explains his/her billing process, gives you reassurance that he/she has handled your type of situation before.

The attorney should stay objective and professional and not make disparaging personal remarks about your ex-spouse. Lawyers who say, "Wow, your ex is really insane!" may be trying too hard to be a buddy. This crosses the line out of a professional relationship.

The attorney's personal commitment to what you feel are the most important issues of your case can be a significant factor in the outcome. For me, that issue was my commitment to a shared-parenting arrangement. Fortunately, the attorney with whom I worked was equally committed to that.

If your divorce escalates into a high-conflict situation, don't be afraid to get a second opinion from another attorney from time to time. Much of what goes on in the legal system may seem contrary to common sense, and you may need reassurance that your case is being handled properly—or confirmation that your instincts are correct and that your case is *not* being handled well.

Your case will be stronger and your attorney will do a better job if you assist by organizing documents, compiling information, monitoring progress, and keeping tabs on your attorney's approach (such as making sure he/she is not using your children as negotiating currency), and prioritizing your "must haves" vs. "wants" vs. "don't care about the lava lamp purchased on the honeymoon." However, on many occasions, you may need to make a leap of faith and trust that your attorney is doing the best job possible for you. This can be very difficult, especially when child custody is an issue.

243

Your attorney should agree to do the following:

➤ send you monthly bills itemizing all expenses and phone calls. If the attorney bills on an hourly basis, you have the right to see the time sheets. (Billing is usually done in increments of six or fifteen minutes, depending on the firm.) You also want to be sure that, whenever possible, the lowest-salaried persons in the office are working on portions of the case that are appropriate for them to handle—in other words, you don't want your attorney typing and filing at $300 per hour;

➤ respond to your phone calls within an hour or so, the same day, or at least within twenty-four hours. If your attorney is in a trial or deposition for another case for a few days, he/she may not be able to respond except to emergencies, but someone in the law office should try to help you in the interim. Do not be offended if your attorney is completely engrossed in someone else's case for a few days. It's a sign that you will probably receive the same level of total commitment from that attorney when your case is in crucial phases;

➤ have contact with opposing counsel once a week or so to be sure the flow of documents between attorneys and accountants is continuing and that all efforts are being made to find grounds for settlement;

➤ report to you immediately after having discussions or correspondence with opposing counsel;

➤ mail you copies of all correspondence and documents sent to or received from opposing counsel and accountant (periodically check the attorney's files on your case to confirm that you have received all correspondence—items can get lost in the mail or may inadvertently not be sent to you), and warn you with a phone call if any of it is inflammatory or insulting;

➤ educate you about the legal process as your case unfolds. ("We are not able to settle on some important issues, and I expect this case will go into formal discovery phase, so there may be depositions taken. Let me tell you what to expect in the next few weeks.") There are two goals here: 1) to help you prepare documents and compile information and 2) to help ease the stress of family law procedures by shining a light into what you may perceive to be a dark, threatening unknown. But there is a limit to how far an attorney can go with emotional reassurance; in other words, do not expect your attorney to be your therapist.

In her book *How to Find the Right Divorce Lawyer*, Robin Page West (an attorney whose own divorce experience with her legal brethren was not always smooth) notes:

> Lawyers, like other people, have their own individual personalities and problems. Nothing distinguishes a lawyer from the rest of humanity except the act of having gone to law school and passing the bar exam. Like any other person, a lawyer can be disorganized, careless, irresponsible, over-committed, vengeful, greedy, addicted, or otherwise undesirable. Like any other person, a lawyer can have ideological perceptions totally different from your own. No state licensing board has screened out undesirable or incompatible lawyers. This is your job and you must do it while enduring the pain of divorce. It won't be easy. It will take guts. But by doing your homework, you should be able to make an educated choice about the lawyer who will play a very important role in how you will live the rest of your life.

245

An attorney friend of mine summed it up this way: "Ultimately, you want someone who is fair-minded and reasonable enough to hammer out a settlement agreement, yet persuasive enough to impress a judge should the need arise."

WORKING WITH YOUR ATTORNEY

Attorneys want your involvement and assistance in some areas of the divorce. Not only will it save you money, but the more your attorney learns about you, the better. A satisfactory result is more expensive and more difficult to achieve when a client simply tells the attorney, "You take care of it."

You and your attorney must be clear with each other about what you are trying to accomplish, then be in philosophical agreement about how to get there.

For instance, if the most important thing is promoting a cooperative shared-parenting arrangement with your ex-spouse, you need to ask yourself if a knock-down, drag-out fight over a $200 difference in monthly support payments will help accomplish that. The answer: probably not.

Be organized with all paperwork. Meet with your attorney every so often and go over the progress of the case. Ask what the next steps are. Find out if you can do anything to make the process cheaper or speedier.

You must move the process along yourself sometimes. Nobody will care as much about your case as you do.

You must tell your attorney the truth about your life situation. Not doing so may result in great damage to your case.

From *How to Find the Right Divorce Lawyer* by Robin Page West:

> The sooner your lawyer knows of the weaknesses in your case, the sooner he can get started developing a plan to overcome them. If the other side has the information and springs it on your lawyer at trial, your lawyer will appear incompetent to the judge. Remember, your spouse knows a lot about your past and will be feeding all sorts of negative information about you to his or her own lawyer. Don't risk your lawyer's credibility (or your own) by withholding potentially damaging information. Better to get everything out in the open so the damage can be controlled.

As I noted earlier in the book, you must use your attorney for legal matters, an accountant for financial matters, and a therapist for emotional matters. Don't get these mixed up.

To a degree, an attorney must be part mental health therapist and try to calm emotionally volatile clients to convince them to take a long-term view of divorce. But it will be more beneficial and less expensive for you to see a therapist to deal with the emotional content of the divorce.

Sometimes attorneys are at the mercy of their clients. The attorney may be retained by a sane-looking client who, after a few weeks, reveals himself to be a rage-filled lunatic. This can be wild ride for the attorney because it isn't easy to "fire" a client.

You may think you can control the way your attorney handles your case. Not likely. It is akin to instructing your surgeon how to perform your heart bypass. When you try to "instruct" your attorney how you want issues handled, you may get a letter that says something like: "I will proceed in the manner in which you have requested. However, this letter is to confirm our phone conversation earlier today in which I strongly advised against taking this course of action."

Such a letter serves as self-protection for the attorney. It is a signal that your anger and vindictiveness may be clouding your judgment; you may be stepping into that zone of "rageful spouse syndrome." It is a first step in the attorney's self-defense measures against a client who, when the case goes sour, may take legal action against the attorney for mishandling the case.

A scapegoating client may (perhaps subconsciously) manufacture himself as a victim of his own attorney. For instance, if an attorney tells a client something he doesn't want to hear about the realities of settlements and judgments, that client may react with self-destructive behavior—having the attorney take unreasonable positions or make exaggerated claims by asking for things to which the client is not entitled. Predictably, most of these clients will be disappointed with the result. But, being scapegoaters, they're not going to take responsibility and admit that they created the situation. Instead they'll say, "It's the lawyer's fault."

248

Working with an attorney—who has other cases that demand his/her attention—can be frustrating. You may want answers or action immediately, but that's not likely to happen often. Sometimes the slow pace can be helpful, though, for many problems resolve themselves over a few days or weeks.

You and your attorney must find a balance: Despite your suspicions about your ex-spouse, you should not assume that all his or her actions are done in bad faith. Much of the confusion in divorce is the result of errors and misunderstandings that do not involve malice. Direct communication and mediation with your estranged spouse can help de-escalate these situations.

Clients can become emotionally invested in an attorney. They may feel, or may be led to believe, that they have finally found the one person in life who understands them, who is their savior from the evil ex-spouse, who is the source of empowerment they've been denied for years. When this happens, errors or unethical actions by the attorney become difficult to challenge. For instance, clients may begin to justify their acceptance of unethical actions by their attorney because:

➤ they fear that the attorney will not respond well to criticism and may not work hard on their case,

➤ they are afraid that dissolving their relationship with the original attorney and starting the case over with a new attorney will place them at a disadvantage in the litigation,

➤ they dread losing face with their friends and ex-spouse by admitting that they made a poor choice.

You want an attorney who shares your values on such issues as shared parenting of your children; you want your attorney to have a personal commitment to your case but not to become emotionally entangled in it. An attorney who loses objectivity loses effectiveness. For this reason, doctors generally don't perform surgery on their own family members.

Don't expect attorneys to create justice or fairness. They can't change the world. What they may be able to do, however, is influence divorce events slightly in your favor, then usher you out the door into your new life.

249

DIVIDING ASSETS

The laws defining the division of assets vary from state to state. (As of this writing, only a few of the fifty states have community-property divorce laws.) This chapter descibes the process in a community-property state (such as California). Hopefully, it will give you some idea of what to expect as your divorce unfolds.

There are generally two types of property to be considered when a marriage dissolves:

1.   Separate Property (nonmarital property): assets (or debts) that each party acquired before and after marriage or individual gifts acquired during the marriage (such as an inheritance). Each party retains his/her own separate property when the marriage ends.

2.   Community Property (marital property): assets (or debts) that were acquired during the marriage and that are to be divided (usually 50/50) between the parties.

This property can be in the form of cash, investments, real estate, rental property, vehicles, automobile, and so on. Portions of separate-property finances (interest income, for example) may be factored into support payment calculations or may be used to fund an equalization payment (defined below).

When you divorce, you will need to proceed with the "equitable distribution" of community property. This means that all marital assets must be defined and valued as of a certain date (it may be date of separation, date of appraisal of a house, or date of division of investments) so that any changes in their value will impact each party equally.

When all of this is done (and it may take months of hard work, negotiation, or litigation), one party makes an "equalization payment" to the other—essentially buying out the other spouse's shares of home, car, furniture, community property debts/assets, and so on.

A positive, productive relationship with mediators, attorneys, and accountants is possible if a couple agrees in principle to bear the losses equitably and neither party is trying to use division of assets as a way to cheat or punish the ex or stay connected to the ex in a negative way.

The laws on division of property after marriage are pretty clear-cut and fair. You may need to make some painful compromises, but don't litigate unless absolutely necessary. The financial and emotional cost of litigation may be high.

The craziness of divorce often makes dividing marital assets an area where a lot of conflict arises as one or both parties may engage in such tactics as:

251

➤ trying to hide financial assets,

➤ removing large sums from marital bank accounts,

➤ removing marital property items from the home, claiming they are separate property,

➤ running up bills on marital credit cards after the date of separation.

Don't use the issue of dividing assets to stay connected to your ex-spouse. Accept the fact that you will be losing some things that are dear to you. A friend of mine reframed the losses of divorce by thinking of them as if the assets had been destroyed in a house fire (keeping in mind that virtually all of these things can be replaced). Keep the division of assets as businesslike as possible. Take a deep breath, accept the losses, and get this divorce finalized so you can move forward with life.

People have a tendency to react to this painful division of assets with "He/she got everything he/she wanted. I was the only one who had to compromise." Keep in mind that, in most cases, the other spouse feels exactly the same way. Remember: A good settlement or judgment is defined as one where both parties walk away unhappy.

Although the laws on division of property are pretty clear, some complicated issues or good-faith differences of opinion may need to be negotiated or even litigated.

In his book *From Courtship to Courtroom*, Jed H. Abraham illustrates the complexities that can arise by using the example of one spouse who purchased a rental property prior to marriage. Is the rental income marital or nonmarital? What if you have used marital funds to pay off part of the mortgage? Or if you used marital funds to upgrade the property?

If either you or your ex-spouse has lost control of the case or is being influenced by an attorney whose philosophy is to "do the absolute maximum" on a case, the list of issues needing substantial negotiation or litigation will get long.

As you prepare to define and value property prior to division, you will need to supply a great many documents to your accountants and attorneys. If one party is not willing to cooperate (or an unethical opposing attorney wants to manufacture that perception), your divorce will probably enter the "formal discovery" phase, which will involve depositions, court filings, and hearings. Needless to say, the billable hours will be adding up.

Though the laws on division of assets vary by state, I recommend purchasing one of the many general divorce workbooks available to get a ballpark idea of what lies ahead for you and your soon-to-be-ex-spouse. These workbooks may be found in the legal section of your bookstore. It will help you get organized and will most likely convince you how important professional legal and/or accounting help is to get this done properly.

How far back you need to go differs for each category and for each state, but here is a partial list to get you started:

➤ deeds and titles to house, cars, boats, etc;

➤ family trust documents, family wills;

➤ professional appraisals of house, appliances, furnishings, artwork, jewelry;

➤ income tax returns (probably for the last three years).

253

You will probably need to provide the following documents for the past year:

➤ pay stubs;

➤ all other sources of income (bank account interest, stock market accounts, rental property, etc.);

➤ mortgage, other loans;

➤ bank account and credit-union account statements;

➤ credit card statements;

➤ copies of bills for routine expenses such as utilities, gardening service, etc. (try to account for every dollar you spend each month);

➤ pension or retirement-fund paperwork;

➤ health insurance and life insurance info and bills.

Organize this well in indexed file folders or three-ring binders with numbered index tabs (perhaps even placing page numbers on them); then make copies for your attorney and soon-to-be-ex. Be open and cooperative with this material, and keep a written record of how you have done so in case your ex or his/her attorney claims otherwise.

Some divorce books advise you to acquire copies of these documents even before you tell your spouse you want a divorce. I wouldn't recommend doing this unless you are convinced that your spouse is going to act in bad faith as your divorce begins; being sneaky may invite a hostile reaction and reciprocal behavior from your spouse. However, if you do decide to make copies, don't let your spouse know you have done so unless he or she acts in bad faith and you are left with no choice but to use those copies to proceed with the divorce.

I guarantee that many of the items you fight over during divorce will not matter one whit in a couple of years. Keep your list of "must haves" as short as possible.

CALCULATING SPOUSAL SUPPORT

Spousal support may also be referred to as "alimony" or "maintenance." The manner in which it is determined varies from state to state, but this chapter should give you a glimpse of what's about to happen in your life.

Calculating spousal-support payments involves comparing the incomes of both spouses and trying to equalize monthly income for a certain length of time, which is determined mainly by the duration of the marriage. The spouse who earns more money will be paying support to the "out spouse" (the one receiving support payments) to equalize their incomes for a period of time and to retain the standard of living for both parties as much as possible.

In California, where I live, spousal-support payments generally last for half the length of the marriage for a union of less than ten years—or until the out spouse remarries, at which point spousal support payments end. For a marriage of ten or more years, termed a "marriage of long duration," spousal-support payments can last for the lifetime of the out spouse, or until his/her remarriage. However, there is some flexibility in this for marriages of ten or fifteen years in duration.

Each state has specific formulas for determining support payments; certain factors can influence the payment amounts, but there is realistically not a whole lot of flexibility in most cases.

Many states use computer programs that quickly calculate recommended or "guideline" support payments (see sample in Appendix D). A divorcing couple can actually meet with a family-law mediator and, by ballparking the numbers, determine the approximate length and amount of support payments within an hour.

If you decide to litigate the issue of spousal support, note that a judge is not obligated to follow these guidelines and may use his/her discretion in determining support. However, the judge may be required to justify the choice to do so in writing the final judgment.

In California, the factors that determine spousal-support payments are spelled out in Family Code 4320:

> In ordering spousal support under this part, the court shall consider all of the following circumstances:

> (a) The extent to which the earning capacity of each party is sufficient to maintain the standard of living established during the marriage, taking into account all of the following:
>
> > (1) The marketable skills of the supported party; the job market for those skills; the time and expenses required for the supported party to acquire the appropriate education or training to develop those skills; and the possible need for retraining or education to acquire other, more marketable skills or employment.
> >
> > (2) The extent to which the supported party's present or future earning capacity is impaired by periods of unemployment . . . incurred during the marriage to permit the supported party to devote time to domestic duties.
>
> (b) The extent to which the supported party contributed to the attainment of an education, training, a career position, or a license by the supporting party.

(c) The ability to pay of the supporting party, taking into account the supporting party's earning capacity, earned and unearned income, assets, and standard of living.

(d) The needs of each party based on the standard of living established during the marriage.

(e) The obligations and assets, including the separate property, of each party.

(f) The duration of the marriage.

(g) The ability of the supported party to engage in gainful employment without duly interfering with the interests of dependent children in the custody of the party.

(h) The age and health of the parties, including, but not limited to, consideration of emotional distress resulting from domestic violence perpetrated against the supported party by the supporting party where the court finds documented evidence of a history of domestic violence, as defined in Section 6211, against the supported party by the supporting party.

(i) The immediate and specific tax consequences to each party.

(j) The balance of the hardship to each party.

(k) The goal that the supported party shall be self-supporting within a reasonable period of time. Except in the case of a marriage of long duration . . . a "reasonable period of time" for purposes of this section generally shall be one-half the length of the marriage. However, nothing in this section is intended to limit the court's discretion to order support for a greater or lesser length of time, based on . . . other factors . . . and the circumstances of the parties.

(l) Any other factors the court determines are just and equitable.

CALCULATING CHILD SUPPORT

Child-support payments are determined by many of the same principles as spousal support: The parents' financial data are compared, and "guideline support payments" are calculated. As with spousal support, family law professionals may enter your financial data into a computer program designed for the purpose of calculating support payments (again, refer to samples in the Appendix).

Many factors or special circumstances can impact child-support payments. These are different for each state but include such considerations as: the amount of custody time children spend with each parent, financial resources of each parent, health of all parties, whether extra expenses (such as education or medical bills) for a child are shared or borne by one parent, and which parent claims the children as a tax deduction.

However, each state's family law code mandates one of two basic methods for calculating guideline child support payments.

The first method, based on **percentage of income**, determines child support amount by calculating a percentage of the payer's (the noncustodial parent's) income per child. This can be based on gross or net income, depending on the state.

For instance, payment guidelines based on a percentage of the noncustodial parent's income would be something like the following: 20% (1 child), 25% (2 children), 32% (3 children), 40% (4 children), 45% (5 children), and 50% (6 or more children). These amounts may be adjusted according to various factors or special circumstances mentioned above.

The second method, based on **combined income** (also referred to as the "Income Shares Model"), determines child support by comparing incomes and custody time of both parents, then assigning each parent a percentage share of the total child support; it is based on the difference between their incomes and the amount of time each spends with the children. The sample in the Appendix is of this type.

Common child-support problems:

➤ Because child-support payments are determined in large part by the amount of time the child spends with each parent, either parent may seek more custody time with children to impact child-support payments in his/her favor.

➤ The payer may hide assets, quit a job, or find a lower-paying job to avoid support payments. In the latter two circumstances, the court will require the payer to prove that the change in employment status was unavoidable or done in good faith.*

➤ The payer may simply not pay, leaving the custodial spouse with the choice of soldiering on alone or becoming mired in litigation and collection efforts. Note that if the payer files for bankruptcy, he/she is still obligated to make support payments.

259

*In one case, a court granted an ex-husband's request to end spousal-support payments by ruling that his decision to forsake all material assets and income in deciding to become a monk was made in good faith.

➤ The receiver may use child-support money for personal enjoyment instead of for the benefit of the children.

➤ Either spouse's remarriage may create friction or resentment regarding support payments between any combination of the new actors in this life drama.

➤ The payer may have other support obligations from one or more previous marriages.

The bottom line is that both parties need to stay focused on the fact that child-support money is for the benefit of the children.

SHARED-PARENTING CUSTODY ARRANGEMENTS

At the outset of divorce, custody arrangements should reflect the level of involvement of each parent before marital separation, with the goal of achieving as close to 50/50 shared parenting as possible.

Parents of preschoolers may resist the idea of young children moving back and forth between homes; the children may reinforce this resistance by crying as they make the transition. However, children often fuss and cry when they transition to day care, preschool, grandparents' homes, or the babysitter's. This is normal (it's called separation anxiety) and may have little or nothing to do with the divorce.

There are many different kinds of custody schedules. For example, a rare type of arrangement called "bird's nest custody" stipulates that, rather than having the children change residences every few days, they remain in the family home seven days a week and the parents move in and out of that home on an alternating schedule.

I know of a divorced couple who exchanged their infant each day; they had arranged their work schedules so one of the parents was always available to be with the child. With a 50/50 joint-custody arrangement initiated at such a young age, it seemed likely this child would regard living in both homes as routine and normal—just as other children learn to accept the routine of transitioning to schools or relatives' homes.

The sample custody schedules later in this chapter may serve as a guideline for you to create a schedule that is workable for your family.

Routine is an important element of successful shared parenting. While there should be room for some flexibility, a fairly strict routine of days, times, and transportation plan can give reassuring predictability and stability to a child and can lessen the chances for misunderstandings between parents. ("I thought YOU were picking Junior up from school today!") Each parent must be able to make plans for noncustody days without too many disruptions in schedule requested by the other parent.

262

Do not allow young children to determine the custody schedule. It is too much responsibility for them, and they can use this inappropriate power to manipulate the parents. Remember that most children would choose not to go to school, would choose to watch cartoons all day, would choose to eat sugar treats as the main course at every meal—but we wouldn't think of letting them make those choices. It's the same with custody schedules. You are the parent.

It is important that both parents do school drop-offs and pickups frequently so that they get to know teachers, other students, and other parents. It is best if a child does not feel that school is one parent's territory.

As noted earlier, if the parents are in a state of high conflict, it may be best to hold child transitions at school or another public place. Child-exchange centers are growing in number around the country. They are a neutral territory—a church or other public building—that is staffed by trained monitors at selected times during the week so that parents may exchange their children in a supervised setting.

Below are some general guidelines for custody schedules organized by children's ages. These assume that the mother is the primary caregiver (if the child is a newborn), the father is the primary wage-earner who has moved out of the family residence, both parents have adequate parenting skills, and both parents wish to be equally involved with their child. These assumptions are based on societal convention; in no way should the guidelines limit you in creating a custody arrangement customized to your family's needs.

INFANT

263

Usually lives with the mother. The father has frequent visits, perhaps every other day. If the father is not welcome in the mother's residence, he bonds with and cares for the child at his house or at a neutral, mutually acceptable residence such as a relative's house. (But others in that household should let him parent the baby. When others take over parenting duties, this can perpetuate the commonly held belief that men are not good caregivers.) Over weekends and holidays, the baby should be spending longer periods in the father's home (where baby has a bed for naps, preparing for overnights in the future).

As a father who was a fully involved caregiver to our babies when I was married (and who has significant flexibility in my work schedule), I write the above paragraph with reservations. I love to change diapers, give baby baths, do bottle feedings and burping, hold a sleeping infant in the crook of my arm, be there when a baby wakes up in the morning. The above schedule would have deprived my children and me of some important bonding, and I'm not sure I could have agreed to it. It is common for infants to stay at a grandparent's house overnight, so staying overnight at a father's house should not be an issue.

TODDLER

In most cases, toddlers still live primarily with the mother but begin to have overnights at the father's house if proper groundwork has been laid. Some child-development experts recommend that one overnight per week for each year of age is a starting point for making decisions. Begin to create more space for the child in the father's house—a playroom, a corner of the family room with a box of toys, dresser for clothing, shelf for books and videos, certainly the child's own bed. The child has a small backpack or bag to carry favorite toys or stuffed animals back and forth between homes. (It's best to have duplicates of these things in each house in case something is left behind at transition.)

PRESCHOOLER (AGES THREE AND FOUR)

Begin working into regular weekly schedule. Children have frequent contact and perhaps longer, uninterrupted stays with each parent. Whatever schedule you choose, consider making a weekly calendar and posting it in each house so that the child can refer to the schedule and get some sense of what's going on. Perhaps the schedule is something like this:

	Mon	Tue	Wed	Thur	Fri	Sat	Sun
Week 1	F-M	M	M-F	F-M	M	M	M-F
Week 2	F-M	M	M-F	F-M	M	M-F	F

(hyphen [-] indicates transition to other parent at school or at home)

or this:

	Mon	Tue	Wed	Thur	Fri	Sat	Sun
Week 1	F[M]	F	F-M	M	M[F]	M	M-F
Week 2	F	F	F-M	M	M	M-F	F

(brackets [ ] denote afternoon or dinnertime visit)

SCHOOL AGE (age six to ten)

The child is able to handle longer stays in each home.

A (3-4-4-3) arrangement over two weeks such as this keeps school days consistent:

	Mon	Tue	Wed	Thur	Fri	Sat	Sun
Week 1	F	F	F-M	M	M	M	M-F
Week 2	F	F	F-M	M	M	M-F	F

Or a (5-2-2-5) arrangement so the child alternates a full weekend with each parent:

	Mon	Tue	Wed	Thur	Fri	Sat	Sun
Week 1	F-M	M	M-F	F	F-M	M	M
Week 2	M	M	M-F	F	F	F	F

Another option is the alternating-weekend arrangement, which assumes Dad is the primary wage-earner and Mom is the primary caretaker at home. While common, this is my least-favorite scheme because it reinforces the concept of "visits" every other weekend with a "secondary" parent who is not involved in the day-to-day life of the child. Moms can resent the plan too—it portrays the father as the weekend "Disneyland Dad" while Mom has to be the weekday homework enforcer. However, it seems a workable option for many parents and children. This schedule typically reverses during summer and winter school holidays.

	Mon	Tue	Wed	Thur	Fri	Sat	Sun
Week 1	F-M	M	M	M[F]	M	M	M
Week 2	M	M	M[F]	M	M-F	F	F

ADOLESCENTS (AGE ELEVEN TO FOURTEEN)

Preferences of children this age should be considered when making the parenting schedule. Children in early adolescence may prefer alternating whole weeks at each house. In late adolescence, they often prefer to begin spending more time at one house with visits to the other.

MID-TEENS (AGE FOURTEEN TO EIGHTEEN)

Teens often choose to live primarily in one home and end the shuttling back and forth. This is commonly the age of total absorption in themselves, school activities, and peer relationships. They can withdraw from both parents, but their choice can hurt the "rejected" parent the most. Do not argue or resist this choice; they may shut you out of their lives even more. Be patient and be available. They will probably increase contact with you when they're older and less self-absorbed.

Below is a sample parenting schedule in a format that often appears in legal documents. Again, customize it to meet your needs.

WEEKLY PARENTING SCHEDULE

Week 1: Child shall be with Mother from Wednesday at 1:00 p.m. to Saturday at 5:00 p.m.
Child shall be with Father from Saturday at 5:00 p.m to Wednesday at 1:00 p.m.

Week 2: Child shall be with Mother from Wednesday at 1:00 p.m. to Sunday at 1:00 p.m.
Child shall be with Father from Sunday at 1:00 p.m to Wednesday at 1:00 p.m.

HOLIDAY AND VACATION SCHEDULES

Holidays shall take priority over regular parenting schedule. Parent receiving child shall pick up child from other home.

The minor child shall be with mother on Mother's Day and with father on Father's Day beginning 9:00 a.m. Sunday to 9:00 a.m. Monday.

Each parent shall have two one-week vacations with minor child each summer.

Choices shall be made:
ODD-NUMBERED YEARS
Mother shall make first choice of week by April 1.
Father shall make first choice of week by April 14.
Mother shall make second choice of week by May 1.
Father shall make second choice of week by May 14.
Selection process shall be reversed on even-numbered years.

HOLIDAY	TIME	EVEN YEARS	ODD YEARS
New Year's Day	Dec 31 at 1:00 p.m. to Jan 1 at 5:00 p.m.	Father	Mother
Easter*	Sat at 5:00 p.m. to Mon at 9:00 a.m.	Mother	Father
Child's birthday (April 17)	April 16 at 5:00 p.m. to April 18 at 9:00 a.m.	Father	Mother
Memorial Day weekend	Fri (or Sun) at 5:00 to Tue at 9:00 a.m.	Mother	Father
July 4th	July 3 at 5:00 p.m. to July 5 at 9:00 a.m.	Father	Mother
Labor Day weekend	Fri (or Sun) at 5:00 to Tue at 9:00 a.m.	Father	Mother
Halloween	After school Oct 31 to Nov 1 at 9:00 a.m.	Mother	Father
Thanksgiving	Wed at 5:00 p.m. to Fri at 9:00 a.m.	Father	Mother
Christmas Eve*	Dec 24 at 1:00 p.m. to Dec 25 at 1:00 p.m.	Father	Mother
Christmas*	Dec 25 at 1:00 p.m. to Dec 26 at 1:00 p.m.	Mother	Father

* or other religious holiday

APPENDIXES

RECOMMENDED READING

One book is unlikely to give you all the information you need to help you understand the steps of your divorce or how to cope with it emotionally. Not only do divorce laws vary from state to state, but each divorce is an individual, unique thing. Trying to pin it down to a few simple steps is virtually impossible.

It may be difficult to read or concentrate when in the turmoil and grief of a divorce, but educating yourself will probably help allay your fears by making the unknown become known. Furthermore, you will do a better job as a parent, a legal client, and an ex-spouse if you are informed (and willing to follow the experts' advice).

There are hundreds of divorce books on the market; I have read a few dozen. From this limited survey, I recommend these six books as essential reading:

Life Lessons: 50 Things I Learned From My Divorce by Beth Joselow, Avon Books, 1994. This book was healing and reassuring for me as my divorce began. It is short, to the point, easy to read, and full of wisdom.

Healing Hearts by Elizabeth Hickey, M.S.W., and Elizabeth Dalton, J.D., Gold Leaf Press, 1997. Contains excellent information, with an emphasis on the impact of divorce on children. The section at the end of Chapter 3 regarding brainwashing of children is outstanding and should be required reading for all divorcing parents. The second half of the book, written by attorney Elizabeth Dalton, explains some of the legal issues of divorce and offers a basic financial worksheet to help you get organized for your divorce.

Nolo's Pocket Guide to Family Law, Nolo Press, and *The American Bar Association Guide to Family Law,* Times Books. These books define legal terms and describing the divorce process. Several financial workbooks for divorce are also available in the legal section of your bookstore. These may be worthwhile if you want to get into more detail than is provided by the financial worksheet found in *Healing Hearts.*

272

Child Custody Made Simple: Understanding the Laws of Child Custody and Child Support by Webster Watnik, Single Parent Press, 2000. This book is superbly researched, well written, well organized, easy to understand. It is excellent reading for all separating parents, especially if they are considering divorce/custody litigation.

How to Find the Right Divorce Lawyer by Robin Page West, J.D., Contemporary Books, 1997. An articulate, intelligent female attorney describes her own nightmarish divorce and the extreme difficulty she had in finding competent legal representation.

The Divorce Handbook by James T. Friedman, Random House, 1984. A bit dated, but I found the question/answer format to be helpful.

Other classic volumes on divorce:

> *The Best Parent Is Both Parents* edited by David L. Levy, Hampton Roads Publishing, 1993. Excerpts from lectures and writings by the leading experts on children and divorce.

> *Mom's House, Dad's House* by Isolina Ricci, Macmillan, 1980.

> *The Joint Custody Handbook* by Miriam Galper Cohen, Running Press, 1991.

If your divorce looks as though it is headed for the high-conflict category, I would recommend—with certain reservations about their tone—the following three books:

> *Joint Custody With a Jerk* by Julie A. Ross, M.A., and Judy Corcoran, St.Martin's Press, 1996.

> *From Courtship to Courtroom* by Jed H. Abraham, Bloch Publishing, 2000. Worst-case scenarios for soon-to-be-ex-husbands.

> *Divorce: A Woman's Guide to Getting a Fair Share* by Patricia Phillips, J.D., and George Mair, Macmillan, 1995. Worst-case scenarios for soon-to-be-ex-wives.

In recent years, a strong Father's Rights movement has emerged to counter what many see as a bias in favor of mothers in child-custody issues. As a result, many books on the market address this. Below are two I found to be fair and reasonable:

> *Father's Rights: Hard Hitting and Fair Advice for Every Father Involved in a Custody Dispute* by Jeffery M. Leving

with Kenneth A. Dachman, Ph.D., Basic Books, 1997. This book is indeed fair. Nothing is said to minimize the importance of mothers, but the authors seek to ensure that the role of fathers is recognized by society and family law as equally important. The tone is restrained and honest.

Custody for Fathers by Carleen Brennan and Michael Brennan, Brennan Publishing, 1999. A candid look at the family law system. The insights offered by the male and female coauthors about the behavior and motives of litigants and family law professionals are excellent.

Books for Young Children:

274

Dinosaur's Divorce: A Guide for Changing Families by Laurene Krasney Brown and Marc Brown, Little, Brown & Company, 1986.

Let's Talk About It: Divorce by Fred Rogers, G.P. Putnam's Sons, 1996.

Mom and Dad Don't Live Together Any More, text by Kathy Stinson, illustrations by Nancy Lou Reynolds, Annick Press, 1984.

Charlie Anderson by Barbara Abercrombie, Aladdin Paperbacks, 1995. A story about a cat who finds love and contentment in two homes.

It's Not Your Fault, Koko Bear: A Read-Together Book for Parents and Young Children During Divorce by Vicki Lansky, Book Peddlers, 1998.

Books for School Age/Adolescent Children:

Divorce Is Not the End of the World: Zoe's and Evan's Coping Guide for Kids, Tricycle Press, 1997. Good insights into a child's view of divorce, with practical suggestions for resolving problems that inevitably crop up.

Emotional Support and Life Wisdom:

When Bad Things Happen to Good People by Harold S. Kushner, Avon, 1994.

Necessary Losses by Judith Viorst, Fireside Books, Simon & Schuster, 1986.

Imperfect Control by Judith Viorst, Fireside Books, Simon & Schuster, 1999.

Put Yourself in Their Shoes: Understanding How Your Children See the World by Barbara F. Meltz, Dell, 1999.

275

Appendix A - Petition for Dissolution of Marriage (California)

ATTORNEY OR PARTY WITHOUT ATTORNEY *(Name, state bar number, and address)*:	FOR COURT USE ONLY

TELEPHONE NO.:   FAX NO.:

ATTORNEY FOR *(Name)*:

SUPERIOR COURT OF CALIFORNIA, COUNTY OF

STREET ADDRESS:

MAILING ADDRESS:

CITY AND ZIP CODE:

BRANCH NAME:

MARRIAGE OF

  PETITIONER:

RESPONDENT:

PETITION FOR	CASE NUMBER:
☐ **Dissolution of Marriage**	
☐ **Legal Separation**	
☐ **Nullity of Marriage** ☐ **AMENDED**	

1. RESIDENCE (Dissolution only) ☐ Petitioner ☐ Respondent has been a resident of this state for at least six months and of this county for at least three months immediately preceding the filing of this *Petition for Dissolution of Marriage.*

2. STATISTICAL FACTS
   - a. Date of marriage: c. Period between marriage and separation
   - b. Date of separation: Years: 0   Months: 0

3. DECLARATION REGARDING MINOR CHILDREN *(include children of this relationship born prior to or during the marriage or adopted during the marriage)*:
   - a. ☐   There are no minor children.
   - b. ☐   The minor children are:

Child's name	Birth date	Age	Sex

    ☐ Continued on Attachment 3b.
   - c. If there are minor children of the Petitioner and Respondent, a completed *Declaration Under the Uniform Child Custody Jurisdiction Act (UCCJA)* (form MC-150) must be attached.
   - d. ☐   A completed voluntary declaration of paternity regarding minor children born to the Petitioner and Respondent prior to the marriage is attached.

4. ☐   **Petitioner requests** confirmation as separate property assets and debts the items listed
   ☐ in Attachment 4   ☐ below:

Item	Confirm to

NOTICE: Any party required to pay child support must pay interest on overdue amounts at the "legal" rate, which is currently 10 percent.

(Continued on reverse)

Form Adopted for Mandatory Use
Judicial Council of California
Rule 1281 [Rev. July 1, 1999]

PETITION
(Family Law)

Family Code, §§ 2330, 3409;
Cal. Rules of Court, rule 1215

276

Appendix A - Petition for Dissolution of Marriage

MARRIAGE OF *(last name, first name of parties)*:	CASE NUMBER:

5. DECLARATION REGARDING COMMUNITY AND QUASI-COMMUNITY ASSETS AND DEBTS AS CURRENTLY KNOWN
   a. ☐ There are no such assets or debts subject to disposition by the court in this proceeding.
   b. ☐ All such assets and debts have been disposed of by written agreement.
   c. ☐ All such assets and debts are listed ☐ in Attachment 5c ☐ below *(specify)*:

6. **Petitioner requests**
   a. ☐ Dissolution of the marriage based on
      (1) ☐ irreconcilable differences. Fam. Code, § 2310(a)
      (2) ☐ incurable insanity. Fam. Code, § 2310(b)
   b. ☐ Legal separation of the parties based on
      (1) ☐ irreconcilable differences. Fam. Code, § 2310(a)
      (2) ☐ incurable insanity. Fam. Code, § 2310(b)
   c. ☐ Nullity of void marriage based on
      (1) ☐ incestuous marriage. Fam. Code, § 2200
      (2) ☐ bigamous marriage. Fam. Code, § 2201

   d. ☐ Nullity of voidable marriage based on
      (1) ☐ petitioner's age at time of marriage. Fam. Code, § 2210(a)
      (2) ☐ prior existing marriage. Fam. Code, § 2210(b)
      (3) ☐ unsound mind. Fam. Code, § 2210(c)
      (4) ☐ fraud. Fam. Code, § 2210(d)
      (5) ☐ force. Fam. Code, § 2210(e)
      (6) ☐ physical incapacity. Fam. Code, § 2210(f)

7. **Petitioner requests** that the court grant the above relief and make injunctive (including restraining) and other orders as follows:

	Petitioner	Respondent	Joint	Other
a. Legal custody of children to	☐	☐	☐	☐
b. Physical custody of children to	☐	☐	☐	☐
c. Child visitation be granted to	☐	☐		☐
(1) ☐ Supervised for	☐	☐		
(2) ☐ No visitation for	☐	☐		
(3) ☐ Continued on Attachment 7c(3).				

   d. ☐ Determination of parentage of any children born to the Petitioner and Respondent prior to the marriage.
   e. Spousal support payable by (wage assignment will be issued) ☐ ☐
   f. Attorney fees and costs payable by ☐ ☐
   g. ☐ Terminate the court's jurisdiction (ability) to award spousal support to respondent.
   h. ☐ Property rights be determined.
   i. ☐ Petitioner's former name be restored *(specify)*:
   j. ☐ Other *(specify)*:
      ☐ Continued on Attachment 7j.

8. If there are minor children born to or adopted by the Petitioner and Respondent before or during this marriage, the court will make orders for the support of the children. A wage assignment will be issued without further notice.

9. **I HAVE READ THE RESTRAINING ORDERS ON THE BACK OF THE SUMMONS, AND I UNDERSTAND THAT THEY APPLY TO ME WHEN THIS PETITION IS FILED.**

I declare under penalty of perjury under the laws of the State of California that the foregoing is true and correct.

Date:

....
(TYPE OR PRINT NAME)

▶ _____
(SIGNATURE OF PETITIONER)

Date:

....
(TYPE OR PRINT NAME)

▶ _____
(SIGNATURE OF ATTORNEY FOR PETITIONER)

NOTICE: Please review your will, insurance policies, retirement benefit plans, credit cards, other credit accounts and credit reports, and other matters you may want to change in view of the dissolution or annulment of your marriage, or your legal separation. However, some changes may require the agreement of your spouse or a court order (see Fam. Code, §§ 231-235). Dissolution or annulment of your marriage may automatically change a disposition made by your will to your former spouse.

1281 [Rev. July 1, 1999]

PETITION
(Family Law)

Page two

Appendix B - Form Interrogatories (California)

ATTORNEY OR PARTY WITHOUT ATTORNEY *(Name and Address)*:	TELEPHONE NO.:
ATTORNEY FOR *(Name)*:	

SUPERIOR COURT OF CALIFORNIA, COUNTY OF

SHORT TITLE OF CASE:

FORM INTERROGATORIES - Family Law	CASE NUMBER:
Asking Party:	
Answering Party:	
Set No.:ˮ	

Sec. 1. Instructions to Both Parties

These interrogatories are intended to provide for the exchange of relevant information without unreasonable expense to the answering party. They do not change existing law relating to interrogatories nor do they affect the answering party's right to assert any privilege or make any objection. **Privileges must be asserted.**

Sec. 2 Definitions

Words in **BOLDFACE CAPITALS** in these interrogatories are defined as follows:

(a) **PERSON** includes a natural person, partnership, any kind of business, legal, or public entity, and its agents or employees.

(b) **DOCUMENT** means all written, recorded, or graphic materials, however stored, produced, or reproduced.

(c) **ASSET or PROPERTY** includes any interest in real estate or personal property. It includes any interest in a pension, profit-sharing, or retirement plan.

(d) **DEBT** means any obligation including debts paid since the date of separation.

(e) **SUPPORT** means any benefit or economic contribution to the living expenses of another person, including gifts.

(f) If asked to **IDENTIFY A PERSON**, give the person's name, last known residence and business address, telephone numbers, and company affiliation at the date of the transaction referred to.

(g) If asked to **IDENTIFY A DOCUMENT**, attach a copy of the document unless you explain why not. If you do not attach the copy, describe the document, including its date and nature, and give the name, address, telephone number, and occupation of the person who has the document.

Sec. 3. Instructions to the Asking Party

Check the box next to each interrogatory you want the answering party to answer.

Sec. 4. Instructions to the Answering Party

You must answer these interrogatories under oath within 30 days, in accordance with Code of Civil Procedure section 2030.

You must furnish all information you have or can reasonably find out, including all information (not privileged) of your attorneys or under your control. If you don't know, say so.

If an interrogatory is answered by referring to a document, the document must be attached as an exhibit to the response and referred to in the response. If the document has more than one page, refer to the page and section where the answer can be found.

If a document to be attached to the response may also be attached to the Schedule of Assets and Debts form, the document should be attached only to the response, and the form should refer to the response.

If an interrogatory cannot be answered completely, answer as much as you can, state the reason you cannot answer the rest, and state any information you have about the unanswered portion.

Sec. 5. Oath

Your answers to these interrogatories must be under oath, dated, and signed. Use the following form *at the end of your answers:*

ˮ I declare under penalty of perjury under the laws of the State of California that the foregoing answers are true and correct.

_____	_____
(DATE)	(SIGNATURE) ˮ

(Continued on reverse)

Form Approved by Rule 1292.10
Judicial Council of California
1292.10 [New July 1, 1990]

FORM INTERROGATORIES
(Family Law)

Code of Civil Procedure, §§ 2030(c), 2033.5

278

☐ 1. **Personal History**. State your full name, current residence address and work address, social security number, any other names you have used, and the dates between which you used each name.

☐ 2. **Agreements**. Are there any agreements between you and your spouse made before or during your marriage or after your separation that affect the disposition of **ASSETS, DEBTS,** or **SUPPORT** in this proceeding? If your answer is yes, for each agreement, state the date made and whether it was written or oral, and attach a copy of the agreement or describe its content.

☐ 3. **Legal Actions**. Are you a party or do you anticipate being a party to any legal or administrative proceeding other than this action? If your answer is yes, state your role and the name, jurisdiction, case number, and a brief description of each proceeding.

☐ 4. **Persons Sharing Residence**. State the name, age, and relationship to you of each **PERSON** at your present address.

☐ 5. **Support Provided Others**. State the name, age, address, and relationship to you of each **PERSON** for whom you have provided **SUPPORT** during the past 12 months and the amount provided per month for each.

☐ 6. **Support Received for Others**. State the name, age, address, and relationship to you of each **PERSON** for whom you have received **SUPPORT** during the past twelve months and the amount received per month for each.

☐ 7. **Current Income**. List all income you received during the past 12 months, its source, the basis for its computation, and the total amount received from each. Attach your last three pay check stubs.

☐ 8. **Other Income**. During the past three years have you received cash or other property from any source not identified in 7? If so, list the source, the date, and the nature and value of the property.

☐ 9. **Tax Returns**. Attach copies of all tax returns and schedules filed by or for you in any jurisdiction for the past three calendar years.

☐ 10. **Schedule of Assets and Debts**. Complete the Schedule of Assets and Debts form served with these interrogatories.

☐ 11. **Separate Property Contentions**. State the facts that support your contention an asset or debt is separate property.

☐ 12. **Property Valuations**. Have you had written appraisals or offers to purchase during the past 12 months on any of the assets listed on your completed Schedule of Assets and Debts. If your answer is yes, **IDENTIFY THE DOCUMENT.**

☐ 13. **Property Held by Others**. Is there any **PROPERTY** held by any third party in which you have any interest or over which you have any control? If your answer is yes, indicate whether the property is shown on the Schedule of Assets and Debts completed by you. If it is not, describe and identify each such asset and state its present value and the basis for your valuation, and **IDENTIFY THE PERSON** holding the asset.

☐ 14. **Retirement and Other Benefits**. Do you have an interest in any disability, retirement, profit sharing, or deferred compensation plan? If your answer is yes, **IDENTIFY** each plan and provide the name, address, and telephone number of the administrator and custodian of records.

☐ 15. **Claims of Reimbursement**. Do you claim the legal right to be reimbursed for any expenditures of your separate or community property? If your answer is yes, state all supporting facts.

☐ 16. **Credits**. Do you claim reimbursement credits for payments of community debts since the date of separation? If your answer is yes, **IDENTIFY** the source of payment, the creditor, the date paid, and the amount paid. State whether you have added to the debt since the separation.

☐ 17. **Insurance.** **IDENTIFY** each health, life, automobile, and disability insurance policy or plan that you now own or that covers you, your children, or your assets. State the policy type, policy number, and name of company. **IDENTIFY** the agent and give the address.

☐ 18. **Health.** Is there any physical or emotional condition that limits your ability to work? If your answer is yes, state each fact on which you base your answer.

☐ 19. **Children's Needs**. Do you contend your children have any special needs? If so, identify the child with the need, the reason for the need, its cost, and its expected duration.

☐ 20. **Attorney Fees**. State the total amount of attorney fees and costs incurred by you in this proceeding, the amount paid, the source of money paid, and describe the billing arrangements.

☐ 21. **Gifts**. List any gifts you have made without the consent of your spouse in the past 24 months, their value, and the recipients.

Appendix C - Income and Expense Declaration (California)

ATTORNEY OR PARTY WITHOUT ATTORNEY *(Name and Address)*:	TELEPHONE NO.:	FOR COURT USE ONLY

ATTORNEY FOR *(Name)*:

SUPERIOR COURT OF CALIFORNIA, COUNTY OF

STREET ADDRESS:

MAILING ADDRESS:

CITY AND ZIP CODE:

BRANCH NAME:

PETITIONER/PLAINTIFF:

RESPONDENT/DEFENDANT:

INCOME AND EXPENSE DECLARATION	CASE NUMBER:

Step 1
Attachments to this summary

I have completed ☐ Income ☐ Expense ☐ Child Support Information forms.
(If child support is not an issue, do not complete the Child Support Information Form. If your only income is AFDC, do not complete the Income Information Form.)

Step 2
Answer all questions that apply to you

1. Are you receiving or have you applied for or do you intend to apply for welfare or AFDC?
   ☐ Receiving ☐ Applied for ☐ Intend to apply for ☐ No
2. What is your date of birth *(month/day/year)*? . . . . _____
3. What is your occupation? _____
4. Highest year of education completed: _____
5. Are you currently employed? ☐ Yes ☐ No
   a. If yes: (1) Where do you work? *(name and address)*: _____

   (2) When did you start work there *(month/year)*? . . . . _____
   b. If no: (1) When did you last work *(month/year)*? . . . . _____
   (2) What were your gross monthly earnings? . . . . _____
6. What is the total number of minor children you are legally obligated to support? . . . . _____

Step 3
Monthly income information

7. Net monthly disposable income *(from line 16a of Income Information)*: . . . . $ _____

8. Current net monthly disposable income *(if different from line 7, explain below or on Attachment 8)*: $ _____

Step 4
Expense information

9. Total monthly expenses from line 2q of Expense Information: . . . . $ _____
10. Amount of these expenses paid by others: . . . . $ _____

Step 5 Other party's income

11. My estimate of the other party's gross monthly income is: . . . . $ _____

Step 6
Date and sign this form

I declare under penalty of perjury under the laws of the State of California that the foregoing and the attached information forms are true and correct.

Date:

▶

. . . . _____
(TYPE OR PRINT NAME)   (SIGNATURE OF DECLARANT)

☐ Petitioner ☐ Respondent

Page one of _____

Form Adopted by Rule 1285.50
Judicial Council of California
1285.50 [Rev. January 1, 1995]

INCOME AND EXPENSE DECLARATION
(Family Law)

Appendix C - Income and Expense Declaration

PETITIONER/PLAINTIFF:		CASE NUMBER:
RESPONDENT/DEFENDANT:		
INCOME INFORMATION OF *(name)*:		

1. Total gross salary or wages, including commissions, bonuses, and overtime paid during the last 12 months: 1. $ _____

2. All other money received during the last 12 months **except welfare, AFDC,** *Specify sources below:*
   SSI, spousal support from this marriage, or any child support. _____ 2a. $ _____
   Include pensions, social security, disability, unemployment, military ba-
   sic allowance for quarters (BAQ), spousal support from a different mar- _____ 2b. $ _____
   riage, dividends, interest or royalty, trust income, and annuities.
   Include income from a business, rental properties, and reimbursement of _____ 2c. $ _____
   job-related expenses.
   ▶ *Prepare and attach a schedule showing gross receipts less cash ex-* _____ 2d. $ _____
   penses for each business or rental property.

3. Add lines 1 through 2d . . . . 3. $ _____
   Divide line 3 by 12 and place result on line 4a.

	Average last 12 months:	Last month:
4. Gross income	4a. $ _____	4b. $ _____
5. State income tax	5a. $ _____	5b. $ _____
6. Federal income tax	6a. $ _____	6b. $ _____
7. Social Security and Hospital Tax ("FICA" and "MEDI") or self-employment tax, or the amount used to secure retirement or disability benefits	7a. $ _____	7b. $ _____
8. Health insurance for you and any children you are required to support	8a. $ _____	8b. $ _____
9. State disability insurance	9a. $ _____	9b. $ _____
10. Mandatory union dues	10a. $ _____	10b. $ _____
11. Mandatory retirement and pension fund contributions . . . . *Do not include any deduction claimed in item 7.*	11a. $ _____	11b. $ _____
12. Court-ordered child support, court-ordered spousal support, and voluntarily paid child support in an amount not more than the guideline amount, **actually being paid for a relationship** *other* **than that involved in this proceeding:**	12a. $ _____	12b. $ _____
13. Necessary job-related expenses *(attach explanation)*	13a. $ _____	13b. $ _____
14. Hardship deduction (Line 4d on Child Support Information Form)	14a. $ _____	14b. $ _____
15. Add lines 5 through 14 . . . . **Total monthly deductions:**	15a. $ _____	15b. $ _____
16. Subtract line 15 from line 4 . . . . **Net monthly disposable income:**	16a. $ _____	16b. $ _____

17. AFDC, welfare, spousal support from this marriage, and child support from other relationships received each month . . . . 17. $ _____
18. Cash and checking accounts: . . . . 18. $ _____
19. Savings, credit union, certificates of deposit, and money market accounts: . . . . 19. $ _____
20. Stocks, bonds, and other liquid assets: . . . . 20. $ _____
21. All other property, real or personal *(specify below)*: . . . . 21. $ _____

▶ **Attach a copy of your three most recent pay stubs.** Page ____ of ____

Form Adopted by Rule 1285.50a
Judicial Council of California
1285.50a [Rev. January 1, 1995]
INCOME INFORMATION
(Family Law)

Divorce: Making the Break

<table>
<tr><td>PETITIONER/PLAINTIFF:</td><td rowspan="3">CASE NUMBER:</td></tr>
<tr><td>RESPONDENT/DEFENDANT:</td></tr>
<tr><td>EXPENSE INFORMATION OF (name):</td></tr>
</table>

1.

		name	age	relationship	gross monthly income
a. List all persons living in your home **whose expenses are included below** and their income: ☐ Continued on Attachment 1a.	1. 2. 3. 4.				
b. List all other persons living in your home and their income: ☐ Continued on Attachment 1b.	1. 2. 3.				

2. MONTHLY EXPENSES

a. Residence payments

  (1) ☐ Rent or ☐ mortgage .... $ _____

  (2) If mortgage, include:

    Average principle ...... $ _____

    Average interest ...... $ _____

    Impound for real property taxes ...... $ _____

    Impound for home-owner's insurance ... $ _____

  (3) Real property taxes (if not included in item (2)) .... $ _____

  (4) Homeowner's or renter's insurance (if not included in item (2)). .... $ _____

  (5) Maintenance .... $ _____

b. Unreimbursed medical and dental expenses .... $ _____

c. Child care .... $ _____

d. Children's education .... $ _____

e. Food at home and household supplies . $ _____

f. Food eating out .... $ _____

g. Utilities .... $ _____

h. Telephone .... $ _____

i. Laundry and cleaning .... $ _____

j. Clothing .... $ _____

k. Insurance (life, accident, etc. Do not include auto, home, or health insurance) $ _____

l. Education (specify): .... $ _____

m. Entertainment .... $ _____

n. Transportation and auto expenses (insurance, gas, oil, repair) .... $ _____

o. Installment payments (insert total and itemize below in item 3) .... $ _____

p. Other (specify): .... $ _____

q. TOTAL EXPENSES (a-p) .... $ _____
(do not include amounts in a(2))

3. ITEMIZATION OF INSTALLMENT PAYMENTS OR OTHER DEBTS ☐ Continued on Attachment 3.

CREDITOR'S NAME	PAYMENT FOR	MONTHLY PAYMENT	BALANCE	DATE LAST PAYMENT MADE

4. ATTORNEY FEES

a. To date I have paid my attorney for fees and costs: $ _____ The source of this money was:

b. I owe to date the following fees and costs over the amount paid:

c. My arrangement for attorney fees and costs is:

    I confirm this information and fee arrangement. ▶ _____

                                   (SIGNATURE OF ATTORNEY)

_____

                         (TYPE OR PRINT NAME OF ATTORNEY)

Page ____ of ____

Form Adopted by Rule 1285.50b
Judicial Council of California
1285.50b [Rev. January 1, 1995]

EXPENSE INFORMATION
(Family Law)

282

Appendix C - Income and Expense Declaration

PETITIONER/PLAINTIFF:	CASE NUMBER:
RESPONDENT/DEFENDANT:	
CHILD SUPPORT INFORMATION OF *(name)*:	

THIS PAGE MUST BE COMPLETED IF CHILD SUPPORT IS AN ISSUE.

1. Health insurance for my children ☐ is ☐ is not available through my employer.
   a. Monthly cost paid by me or on my behalf for the children *only* is: $ _____
      Do not include the amount paid or payable by your employer.
   b. Name of carrier:
   c. Address of carrier:

   d. Policy or group policy number:

2. Approximate percentage of time each parent has primary physical responsibility for the children:
   Mother ____ % Father ____ %

3. ☐ The court is requested to order the following as additional child support:
   a. ☐ Child care costs related to employment or to reasonably necessary education or training for employment skills
      (1) Monthly amount currently paid by mother: $
      (2) Monthly amount currently paid by father: $
   b. ☐ Uninsured health care costs for the children *(for each cost state the purpose for which the cost was incurred and the estimated monthly, yearly, or lump sum amount paid by each parent)*:

   c. ☐ Educational or other special needs of the children *(for each cost state the purpose for which the cost was incurred and the estimated monthly, yearly, or lump sum amount paid by each parent)*:

   d. ☐ Travel expense for visitation
      (1) Monthly amount currently paid by mother: $
      (2) Monthly amount currently paid by father: $

4. ☐ The court is requested to allow the deductions identified below, which are justifiable expenses that have caused an extreme financial hardship.

		Amount paid per month	How many months will you need to make these payments
a. ☐	Extraordinary health care expense *(specify and attach any supporting documents)*:	$ _____	_____
b. ☐	Uninsured catastrophic losses *(specify and attach supporting documents)*:	$ _____	_____
c. ☐	Minimum basic living expenses of dependent minor children from other marriages or relationships who live with you *(specify names and ages of these children)*:	$ _____	_____
d.	Total hardship deductions requested *(add lines a - c)*:	$ _____	

Page _____ of _____

Form Adopted by Rule 1285.50c
Judicial Council of California
1285.50c [Rev. January 1, 1995]

CHILD SUPPORT INFORMATION
(Family Law)

ATTACHMENT TO
INCOME & EXPENSE DECLARATION

(Page 3 - Continued)

CREDITOR NAME	PAYMENT FOR	MONTHLY PAYMENT	BALANCE	DATE LAST PAYMENT MADE

Total: _____ _____

Appendix D - Sample DissoMaster® Support Calculation (California)

DissoMaster® reproduced by permission of the California Family Law Report, Inc.

2001	Formal Report	Monthly figures

Figures on this page exclude effects of guideline support.

		Father	Mother
CHILDREN			
Supported children of this relationship		0	1
Husband's visitation of children with wife		49 %	
Wife's visitation of children with husband			0 %
INCOME			
Tax filing status		SINGLE	HH/MLA
Number of federal exemptions		1	2
Wage and salary income		6000	3000
Self-employment income		0	0
Other federally taxable income		21	21
Other non-taxable income		0	0
TOTAL GUIDELINE INCOME		6021	3021
TANF and child support received from other relationships		0	0
New spouse income on joint return		0	0
EXPENSES			
Deductible support paid re other relationships	B	0	0
Non-deductible support paid re other relationships	G	0	0
Health insurance premiums	B	0	0
Recurring other medical, dental and drug expenses	T	0	0
Recurring property taxes paid	T	0	0
Recurring interest expense	T	0	0
Recurring charitable contribution deductions	T	0	0
Recurring miscellaneous expenses	T	0	0
Union dues required for employment	B	0	0
Mandatory retirement/pension contributions	B	0	0
Hardship deductions	G	0	0
Other discretionary guideline deductions	G	0	0
Child care expenses, this relationship	B	0	0
Total guideline deductions, excluding taxes		0	0
COMPUTATIONS (BEFORE SUPPORT)			
State income tax (prorated in the case of MFJ)		359	13
Federal income tax (prorated in the case of MFJ)		1228	259
FICA		459	230
Federal self-employment tax		0	0
State employment taxes		27	21
Total taxes		2072	523
TOTAL GUIDELINE DEDUCTIONS		2072	523
NET GUIDELINE INCOME BEFORE SUPPORT		3949	2498

DissoMaster(tm) V.2000-1-CA   *Page 2*

2001   **Formal Report**   **Monthly figures**

Guideline spousal support is based on adjusted nets

	Guideline	Proposed
COMBINED CASH FLOW		
Combined net spendable income	6495	6600
Percent change	0 %	2 %
FATHER'S CASH FLOW		
After-tax cost (-) or benefit (+) of payment	-474	-418
Net spendable income after support	3474	3531
Percent of combined net spendable income	53 %	53 %
Percent of total tax savings	0 %	54 %
Total taxes after credits	1970	1626
Value of dependency exemptions	67	109
Number of withholding allowances	2	6
Net wage paycheck	3920	4224
State marginal bracket	9 %	9 %
Federal marginal bracket	28 %	28 %
Combined marginal bracket	35 %	35 %

286

	Guideline	Proposed
MOTHER'S CASH FLOW		
After-tax cost (-) or benefit (+) of payment	523	571
Net spendable income after support	3020	3069
Percent of combined net spendable income	47 %	47 %
Percent of total tax savings	0 %	46 %
Total taxes after credits	577	815
Value of dependency exemptions	78	67
Number of withholding allowances	3	0
Net wage paycheck	2410	2203
State marginal bracket	6 %	6 %
Federal marginal bracket	15 %	28 %
Combined marginal bracket	20 %	32 %

Appendix D - Sample DissoMaster® Support Calculation

2001   **Formal Report**   **Monthly figures**

Guideline spousal support is based on adjusted nets

Support Summary

GUIDELINE SUPPORT

Child care	0	
Child support	294	father pays mother
Spousal support	282	father pays mother
Total support	576	father pays mother

PROPOSED SETTLEMENT

Non-deductible support	0	
Deductible support	863	father pays mother
Total support	863	father pays mother

Comments

On page 1, the lines marked G affect guideline directly, lines marked T affect taxes directly and guideline indirectly through changes in tax, and lines marked B affect both guideline and taxes directly.

Proposed column minimizes taxes, then splits the enlarged net spendable income in the same proportion as the guideline allocation.

Proposed column assumes that Mother releases 1 exemptions via IRS Form 8332.

Spousal Support formula: S.Clara SS

Tax year: 2001

Appendix E

Common Provisions of the Separation Agreement

The purpose of a separation agreement is to spell out the agreed-upon rights and responsibilities of each member of a divorcing couple. The exact terms will vary from state to state and from couple to couple, depending on their circumstances, but here, intended as examples only, are some terms many of them have in common.

Obviously each separation agreement will differ depending on the couples circumstances, and the outline here is not intended to substitute for legal advice tailored to the needs of the parties. The purpose is rather to introduce provisions that may be included in a separation agreement, so that they are not entirely unfamiliar when a couple is presented with one for the first time. The other purpose is to show the degree of flexibility and civility that a separation agreement allows a divorcing couple, compared with most court-ordered arrangements.

I. Introduction: The first part may contain "recitals," meaning a short statement of the facts underlying the agreement, such as: the date of the marriage; the names and birth dates of the children (if any); whether there was a prenuptial agreement, and, if so, the fact that the separation agreement is intended to supersede the prenup; the fact that irreconcilable differences have arisen; and the statement that the couple wishes to live apart from each other for the rest of their lives, and wish to make provisions for all aspects of their respective marital rights and obligations, including property distribution, spousal support, child support, and custody arrangements.

II. Separation: The next section may set forth that the couple agrees to live apart from each other, free of each other's interference or control, as if they were single.

III. Distribution of Property: Next, the agreement might set forth the agreement of the parties regarding property distribution, which is typically done in accordance with state law. Often the most significant asset is the marital home, and the agreement would specify who will own it, who will live there and when, whose name(s) will be on the mortgage, who pays for taxes and upkeep, and, if it is to be sold eventually, provisions for determining acceptable sale price, timing, and split of proceeds. Other property, such as a professional license or a stream of payments (royalties, lottery winnings, and such), will receive somewhat more complex treatment (for example, payments spread out over time or a lump-sum payment signifying the "present value" of the expected stream of income). Typically the disposition of such lesser items as household furnishings, the contents of bank and brokerage accounts, and personal effects is not spelled out in the agreement but is left to the parties to work out prior to the signing of the agreement.

IV. Child Custody: This is often the thorniest area for a divorcing couple to work out without a court order. But often the most satisfactory and enforceable agreements come from the parties them-

290

selves. Following is some sample language from a custody agreement in which the couple agrees that the custody will be joint:

1. The parties shall share joint custody of the Child. The parties acknowledge that each of them has a sound and healthy relationship with the Child, and the parties recognize the importance to each other and to the Child of maintaining such relationships unimpaired. In order to maintain and foster the existing sound and healthy parental relationship of each party to the Child, the parties acknowledge and agree upon the following general principles, which shall guide them in their exercise of their joint custodial rights and responsibilities as hereinafter set forth:

(a) Each party will promote an affectionate relationship between the Child and the other party. Neither party shall, either directly or indirectly, influence the Child so as to prejudice him/her against the other party.

(b) Each party has an equal right and responsibility to share in all basic decisions concerning the upbringing of the Child. The parties shall advise and consult with each other and shall jointly determine all matters concerning the Child's health, education, religious training, welfare, and upbringing. These issues include but are not limited to the selection of schools, camps, colleges, physicians, dentists, psychotherapists, counselors, and other professionals and institutions.

(c) Each party has joint right and entitlement to have physical access to and companionship of the Child, and the Child has the right and entitlement to joint physical access to and companionship of each party.

(d) Despite the dissolution of their marital relation, the parties shall remain partners in the upbringing and education of the Child during the period of the Child's minority, and it is in the best interest of the Child that the parties exercise their joint custodial rights and responsibilities in a spirit of good faith, cooperation, and mutual love for the Child.

2. The parties shall reside within a radius of thirty miles of [location] for so long as the Child is not emancipated as defined herein.

3. The parties make the following provisions for residence of the Child:

(a) The specific vacation and holiday periods to be spent by the Child with either party shall be decided jointly by the parties at the beginning of each year. If the parties are unable to reach agreement within sixty days prior to the start of any such vacation or holiday period, the Husband shall have the first choice of such vacation and holiday periods in odd-numbered years and the Wife shall have the first choice in even-numbered years, such choice to be exercised by written notice to the other party.

(b) During any period when the Child is staying with one of the parties, the other party shall be entitled to reasonable telephone calls and other communications with the Child.

(c) The parties shall divide evenly the time and expense of transporting the Child for the purpose of effectuating the residential arrangements set forth herein.

4. Failure of either party to exercise in whole or in part his or her various rights to share the Child's time as herein provided shall

not constitute a waiver of said party's right to insist thereafter upon compliance with the provisions hereof.

5. Each party shall see to it that the terms "Mother" and "Father" and their derivatives, as used by the Child, shall be reserved as designations only for the parties to this agreement and for no other persons. Notwithstanding any remarriage of the Wife, the Child shall continue to be known under the Husband's surname.

6. Each of the parties agrees to keep the other informed of his or her home and business addresses and telephone numbers. Each party shall keep the other apprised of the whereabouts of the Child while the Child is residing or traveling with him or her.

7. If the Child becomes seriously ill or injured, the party with whom the Child is then staying shall promptly give notice thereof to the other party. In case of serious illness, both parties shall have the absolute right of prompt visitation at the place of the Child's confinement.

8. Each party shall be entitled to complete and full information from any physician, dentist, teacher, camp counselor, psychologist, psychiatrist, psychotherapist, consultant, specialist, or other person attending the Child for any reason whatsoever, and to have copies of any and all reports given by them, or any of them, to either party. Either party, at the request of the other, shall furnish written consent to all such schools, camps, teachers, counselors, physicians, and other specialists authorizing them to send copies of all reports to the other parent and/or to make all such reports and records available to the other party.

9. Each party shall have the right to be in attendance at school, camp, social, athletic, or extracurricular events, including but not limited to graduation, academic honors or achievements, plays, athletic activities, and any other or similar events.

10. In the event of the death of either party before the Child is emancipated, sole custody shall be awarded to the surviving party.

V. Child Support: There are as many different ways to divide financial responsibility for child support as there are divorcing couples. Following is one example in which the couple agreed that the husband would pay sixty percent and the wife forty percent (the ratio of their incomes):

CHILD SUPPORT

1. (a) The Husband and the Wife, in a ratio of 60:40 respectively, shall divide financial responsibility for the support and maintenance of the Child:

(i) the Child's reasonable medical, health insurance, psychotherapy, and dental expenses;

(ii) the Child's reasonable education expenses, including private school and college tuition, fees, uniforms, equipment required by the institution, room and board, books, and transportation;

(iii) the Child's reasonable expenses for tutoring, enrichment programs, lessons, extracurricular activities, religious instruction, and summer camp.

(b) The payments required under Paragraph 1 of this Article V shall continue until the earliest to occur of (i) an "Emancipation Event" as defined and set forth in Article V hereof; or (ii) the death of either of the parties.

2. (a) Until such time as the Child enters school on a full-time basis:

(i) The parties shall jointly employ a child-care provider for the Child; and

(ii) The Husband shall pay to the child-care provider wages [day-care fees] in the amount of [$] per month for the care of the Child; the Wife shall pay the balance of the child-care provider's wages [day-care fees], if any;

(b) The parties' obligations to contribute to the wages of and pay the taxes of such child-care provider [or day-care center] shall terminate at such time as the Child enters school on a full-time basis. After such time, each party shall be free to employ such child-care providers as and to the extent said party sees fit; and each party shall be solely responsible for the wages and taxes payable as a consequence of said party's employment of child-care providers.

3. (a) The parties agree to maintain or cause to be maintained in full force and effect, at each of their respective full and sole expense, one or more life insurance policies for the benefit of the other, for the purpose of ensuring that his or her obligations pursuant to this agreement are satisfied, in the following face amount: [life insurance sufficient to cover any payments listed in agreement] for the years [specify years]. The parties' obligation to maintain

295

such policies shall begin with the execution and delivery of the agreement and shall continue until such time as the parties have fulfilled their respective obligations to the other pursuant to those provisions.

(b) On an annual basis, upon the request of the other, each party shall furnish proof of the existence and status of the life insurance policy/policies described above. If either party is obligated, because of the other's default, to make premium payments on the insurance policy(ies) contemplated in this Paragraph in order to keep it (them) in full force and effect, he or she shall have the right to have such premium payments reimbursed to him or her by the other party on demand.

VI. Spousal Maintenance: The parties may agree that the spouse with greater means or education will provide support payments to the other for a specified duration, while the other spouse develops such skills or educational background needed to become self-supporting. Such provision should also take account of the parties' needs for medical insurance. If the parties agree that no such spousal maintenance is necessary or appropriate, they should say so in the agreement, to avoid future problems.

VII. Income Taxes: Since spouses often file taxes jointly during their marriage, the Separation Agreement will usually spell out what happens after the divorce. Oftentimes, tax provisions can be worked out between cooperative divorcing spouses that result in tax savings to both of them that would not be available to them if they remain "at war" (or if a judge decides the financial arrangements). A qualified tax advisor can give specifics. At a minimum, the separation agreement will state that the parties will file separately from now on; which spouse will claim the child as a dependent; that for any past year in which a joint return was filed and for which the couple may eventually be audited, the parties agree to cooperate with each other, and the spouse who will be handling the audit will be authorized by the other spouse to act in the best interests of both; and the disposition of any refund or further taxes due.

VIII. Debts: The Separation Agreement should spell out what if any debts they have outstanding to third parties (mortgages, car payments, student loans, credit card debt, personal loans) and provide which party will be responsible for which. If there are none, the parties should so state.

IX. Legal Boilerplate: There will be plenty of this in any agreement prepared by a lawyer, and a separation agreement is no exception. Some of it may include: waiver of estate rights, which means that each party agrees not to contest the will of the soon-to-be former spouse or make any claim against his/her estate when he/she dies; who pays for whose legal and accounting fees in connection with the divorce proceedings, or that each party will bear his/her own; and that each party has had the opportunity to review the agreement with a lawyer of his/her choosing and is signing freely and voluntarily.

297